IMAGES
of America

VANISHING
PHOENIX

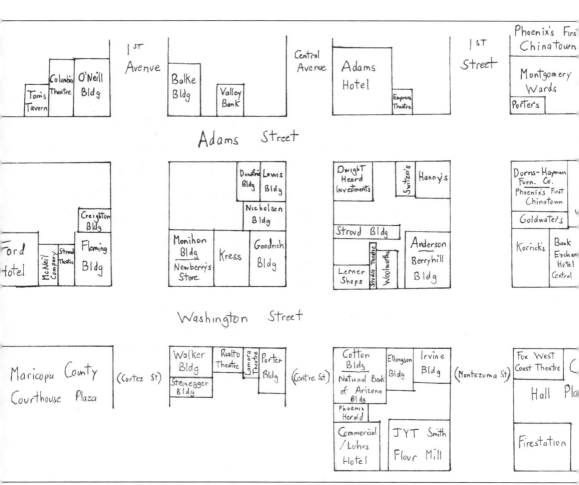

Pictured are the locations of buildings that have vanished from Phoenix's downtown core. (Courtesy Melikian collection.)

On the Cover: The Anderson Building was on the northwest corner of Washington and First Streets in downtown Phoenix. An example of a great Phoenix building, its two huge towers made it a very distinct building. It was built before 1889, and it is pictured here in the late 1890s. Bernard Hayman had his successful furniture store in the building before he joined with C. D. Dorris, forming the Dorris-Hayman Furniture Company, one of the largest stores of its kind in the territory. In 1893, Phoenix had given out a contract for 25 electric streetlights, one of which you can see in this photograph. The building was altered but survived past 1983. (Courtesy McLaughlin Collection, ASU.)

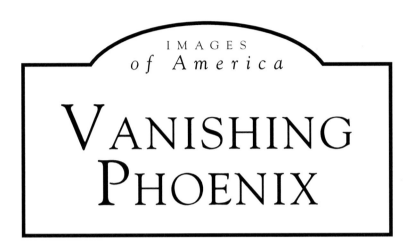

IMAGES
of America

VANISHING PHOENIX

Robert A. Melikian

ARCADIA
PUBLISHING

Published by Arcadia Publishing
Charleston, South Carolina

Printed in the United States of America

Library of Congress Control Number: 2009934027

For all general information contact Arcadia Publishing at:
Telephone 843-853-2070
Fax 843-853-0044
E-mail sales@arcadiapublishing.com
For customer service and orders:
Toll-Free 1-888-313-2665

Visit us on the Internet at www.arcadiapublishing.com

This book is dedicated to my wife, Nevine, who inspires me to remember what the important things in life are and how lucky I am to have found her. This book is also dedicated to improving the City of Phoenix's Historic Preservation Ordinance.

CONTENTS

ACKNOWLEDGMENTS

A nation which does not know what it was yesterday, does not know what it is today, nor what it is trying to do.

—Woodrow Wilson

The Arizona School of Music
The Fleming Building
The Cotton Building
The Fox Theater
The Monihon Building
The John T. Dennis House

The Patton Opera House
The Coffee Pot
The Goodrich Building
The Clark Churchill House
The Anderson Building
The Commercial Hotel

The beauty that was Phoenix. These are some of the names of buildings lost in history. I've tried to identify all the buildings that I could find photographs of, and to investigate the year built and the year lost of each building. You will see the craftsmanship, the art, the charm, the magnificent attention to detail—that's what Phoenix produced in the past. All with a sense of pride and humanity, and all built on a human scale. They welcomed people and produced great memories. They encouraged people to interact and encouraged pedestrian activity. Phoenix had buildings that were good for business and good for neighborhoods. Nature and other people were much more a part of people's lives. These buildings live now only in our memories.

All of the buildings in this book have vanished. Almost all of them were deliberately razed. In most cases, someone decided that the "highest and best use" of the land they sat on was for something else. And now we have to live with those decisions. Perhaps the concept of highest and best use should have included the social or community benefit of the structure along with the immediate economic profit to the temporary owner.

I want to deeply thank the usual suspects: Jared Jackson and Hannah Carney of Arcadia Publishing, who walked me through the book and did the technical wizardry. Pam Rector, archivist at the Phoenix Museum of History, Robert Spindler and Karrie at Arizona State University Archives/McLaughlin Collection, and Marie Hernandez at the Phoenix Public Library, who all gave me images and were great to work with. John Jacquemart, the historic researcher extraordinaire, knows his historic facts better than anyone and was my consultant and coffee drinking buddy.

INTRODUCTION

The U.S. territory of Arizona was officially organized on February 24, 1863, when Pres. Abraham Lincoln signed it into law. Previously during the Civil War, on February 14, 1862, Jefferson Davis had created by proclamation the Confederate territory of Arizona—exactly 50 years to the day before Arizona was to become a state. Pres. William Howard Taft approved Arizona's statehood on February 14, 1912.

To protect the growing number of prospectors and miners that were coming into the newly formed territory, U.S. Army Post Camp Verde (changed to Fort McDowell in 1879) was established on the west bank of the Verde River approximately 6 miles above its confluence with the Salt River. John Y. T. Smith (Y. T. stood for Yours Truly) is credited with seeing the wild hay growing and setting up a hay camp along the north bank of the Salt River approximately 35 miles from Camp McDowell in 1867. John W. "Jack" Swilling saw the potential of the prehistoric canal system and started to develop it in the winter of 1867–1868. In 1870, the 240 residents in the area voted to establish a town on the site we now know of as downtown. It was on cleared, flat ground, above the seasonal floodplain to protect it from flooding, and located about a mile north of the Salt River. The town of Phoenix was initially 1 mile long, a half mile wide, and contained 96 blocks and 320 acres. Resident Darrell Duppa, a Cambridge graduate, reportedly said, "Let's call it Phoenix, for here, on the ruins of the old, a new city will arise," according to the 1892 Phoenix City Directory. By 1874, lots were selling for $7–$11 each, and there were 16 saloons, 4 dance halls, 2 monte banks, and 1 faro table.

At first, the buildings were principally constructed of adobe. Then a local brick kiln was established in 1878 and brick became the material of choice because of its strength and fireproof quality. Completion of the railroad to Maricopa in 1879 and the transcontinental railroad through Arizona in 1883 and 1884 made wood, plate glass, stone, prefabricated items, and pressed and cast metal available for use in constructing Phoenix's early buildings. According to Gerald A. Doyle and Associates in the Roosevelt Neighborhood Historic Buildings Survey, Phoenix residents wanted to provide themselves with the comforts of the cities from which they came and to create the appearance necessary for a "real" town, so the new settlers hastened to discard the use of native materials to create architecture that resembled the rest of America. Thus, architecture in the Queen Anne, Eastlake, Shingle, High Victorian Italianate, and late Second Empire styles began appearing, albeit in simpler versions than their eastern counterparts. Floods, which occurred in 1890 and 1891, changed the pattern of growth, which from then on went north for those who had the money.

Despite occasional natural disasters and setbacks in the national and local economies, Phoenix began the growth that has continued to this day. The early events that were the foundation for this growth were the completion of the 44-mile Arizona Canal, which opened up an additional 100,000 acres of desert to potential agricultural development; construction of a railroad to Phoenix in 1887; an urban railway system, started in 1887; a prosperous local agricultural economy that produced products in commercial quantities; organized promotional efforts, especially by the newspapers and the Phoenix Board of Trade (1888); the establishment of Phoenix as the territorial capital in 1889; the passage of the National Reclamation Act in 1902; and the organization of valley farmers as the Salt River Valley Water Users Association. These last two events were necessary for the construction of Roosevelt Dam, which solved the valley's water problem.

The economy of Phoenix was initially based on agriculture. Businesses and industries were then created to serve the booming agricultural interests and were dependent on the success of irrigation farming. These included hardware and building supply companies, mercantile establishments, real estate firms, banks and loan companies, hay and grain storage warehouses, agricultural implement and machinery companies, and railroads.

The need for diversity became apparent after a series of droughts. Boosterism started to focus on the local climate and health, then tourism. Phoenix began to attract people and grow: 29,000 lived here in 1920; 48,000 in 1930; and 65,000 in 1940. A turning point came in 1940. The city had gone far with farming, a healthcare center, and then a distribution center, but when the war hit the United States, Phoenix turned rapidly into an industrial city. Luke Field, Williams Field, and Falcon Field brought thousands of men into Phoenix. When the war ended, many of these men returned to Phoenix looking for work. Large industry, learning of this labor pool, started to move branches to the area.

The era, commencing with 1940, marked the end of agriculture's role as the area's chief provider. It was the beginning of greater prosperity than Phoenix had ever known through industry and skilled labor. In 1950, Phoenix had 105,000 people, with thousands more living in adjacent communities. In 1970, the population was 584,303 people, almost six times the 1950 population. The population now is around 1.3 million people.

HISTORIC PRESERVATION

Phoenix has not done a great job when it comes to preserving its historic buildings. Consider, for example, that of the 143 historic commercial buildings that miraculously survived until 1984, 55 of them, or 40 percent, have been destroyed in the past 25 years. Business sentiment is not very sympathetic to preservation, and the city's historical preservation ordinance offers very little protection, only a 365-day demolition delay at most. As a result, we have lost almost all of our commercial buildings, including every one in this book. Many historic residential neighborhoods have thankfully remained intact, but this was accomplished strictly on a voluntary basis. Without cooperative owners, there was no preservation in Phoenix. In fact, of the cities that have historic preservation ordinances in the United States, about half of them decided that they can absolutely deny demolition when appropriate—Phoenix has rejected this approach.

Our weak historical preservation ordinance probably comes from our past. Phoenix was built by strong men who came here to make a better life for themselves. It takes a strong man to improve his circumstances and move his family to a place like Phoenix. The city was created by these strong men, but there is a downside. The past is not a big priority for these forward-thinking men. This has resulted in a weak ordinance.

But some things are so important that they need all of us to protect them. Historic buildings are one of those things that improve the quality of life for all of us and teach everyone so much that we should think twice before allowing one to be destroyed. It seems that keeping historic buildings standing is one of the necessary things our government can do to make life better for all of us.

One

LOST BUILDINGS

We shape our buildings; thereafter, our buildings shape us.

—Winston Churchill

HISTORIC PHOENIX COMMERCIAL PROPERTIES SURVEY (1984)		
Name	Address	Constr. Date
Piggly Wiggly Grocery Store	1402-1406 E. Washington	1929
High Class Food Company	1410 E. Washington	ca. 1934
Walter Dubree Building Supplies	1146 E. Van Buren	1925
Phoenix Costume House	1229 E. Washington	1919
Bienvenidos House / Drug Store	1202 E. Jefferson	1929
AZ Citrus Growers Warehouse	616 E. Jackson	1937
Lamb Hotel / Coronado Hotel	807 N. 1st St.	1932
Holohan Grocery	326 N. 4th St.	ca. 1918
Espinoza Grocery and Residence	235 S. 2nd St.	ca. 1900
Central Wholesale Terminal	315 E. Madison / 227 S. 3rd St.	1930
Lightning Delivery Company Warehouse	425 E. Jackson	1915-1917
Portland Lodging House / Adams Annex / Annex Hotel	515 N. Central	ca. 1898
Nielson Radio & Sporting Goods	621 N. Central	1927
Baker & Bayless Grocery	506-508 N. Central	1912
United States Rubber Co. / Messenger Printing	339 N. 1st Ave.	1927
R.D. Roper Building	402 N. Central	1920
Stroud Building	25 N. Central	1900
Wharton Block	36-40 N. Central	1893
Donofrio Building	42 N. Central	1913
Lewis Block	46 N. Central	1901-1902
Winters Building / Craig Building	39 W. Adams	1931
Ellingson Building	19 E. Washington	1899
Crane Plumbing Supply Warehouse	233 S. 1st Ave.	1926
People's Freight Lines	440 S. 1st Ave.	1928
W.A. Webber Building / AZ Trade Bindery	307-311 W. Monroe	1920
Manufacturing Stationers, Inc.	325 W. Adams	ca. 1919
Moore & McLellan Mortuary / A.L. Moore & Sons Mortuary	333 W. Adams	1911-1925
Patton's Grand Theater / Dorris Opera House / Elks Club & Theater / Apache Theater	332 W. Washington	1898
J.W. Walker Building / Central AZ Light & Power Company	10 N. 3rd Ave. / 300 W. Washington	1920
IOOF Hall	245 W. Adams	1920
Orpheum Theater	209 W. Adams	1927
Armour Company	247 W. Jackson	1912
Barrow's Furniture Company Warehouse	305 S. 2nd Ave.	1925
Lescher Warehouse / Maricopa Creamery Co.	305 W. Madison	1930
T.J. Richardson Grocery	609 S. Central	ca. 1910
Higuera Grocery	923 S. 2nd Ave.	1916
Cate Drugs	1001 S. Central	1928
Leong Quong & Company General Merchandise	902 S. Central	1917
Cargill Restaurant / Kunitaro Cheno Restaurant	616 W. Van Buren	1924
Five Points Cash Grocery / A.J. Bayless #1	620 W. Van Buren	1927
Overland AZ Company	12 N. 4th Ave.	ca. 1920
Safeway Pay'n Takit Bakery	208 S. 4th Ave.	1928
Sunrise Tool & Mfg.	476 W. Madison	ca. 1930

Here is a partial list of some of the historic commercial buildings that were demolished not long ago. These buildings lasted into modern times, but then it was decided that there were better uses for the land. The City of Phoenix Historic Preservation Office does its best to identify historic properties, educate the public, and save buildings, but businesses do not appreciate the value of these buildings, so there is little legal protection available. There are a couple buildings in this list that are still standing. (Courtesy City of Phoenix Historic Preservation Office.)

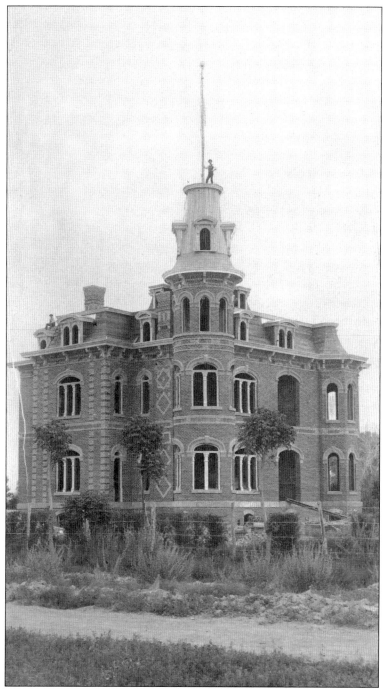

The magnificent Clark Churchill House was on the north side of Van Buren Street, between 5th and 7th Streets. Here it is being completed in 1895 with a proud worker standing on the tower and one sitting on the left side of the roof. This was the image that inspired this book. The author came across this photograph while researching another book and did not know that such a beautiful building ever existed in Phoenix. Perhaps others will be interested in knowing what historic buildings Phoenix had and lost. (Courtesy Phoenix Museum of History.)

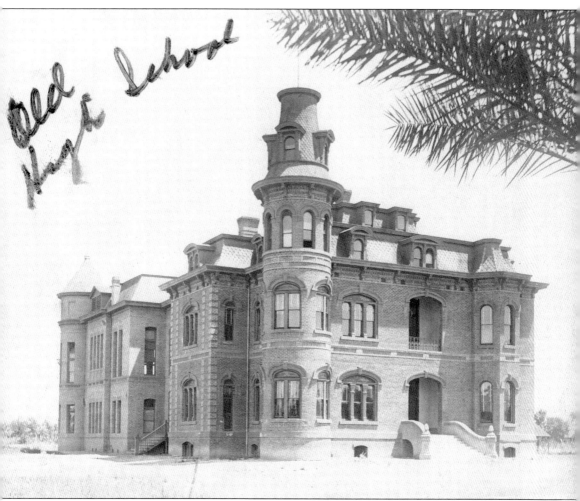

Clark Churchill was an early Phoenix real estate developer, and he was responsible for the Churchill Addition Neighborhood (1888) just north of downtown. His large advertisement on the back cover of the 1892 Phoenix City Directory read: "The Churchill Addition Contains the Best and Most Eligible Building Sites in Phoenix. Good Neighborhood and Within A Short and Pleasant Walk Of The Heart Of The City." However, there was a national depression in 1893, and even though he built this house for himself and his wife, Virginia, to move into, he sold the house along with 6 blocks of land in 1897 to the city for the start of Phoenix Union High School. The huge Victorian-style house adapted to its high school use by an addition to the north, pictured here on the left side of the house. The school was enjoyed by Phoenix students for over 50 years, until it was torn down in 1949. (Courtesy Phoenix Museum of History.)

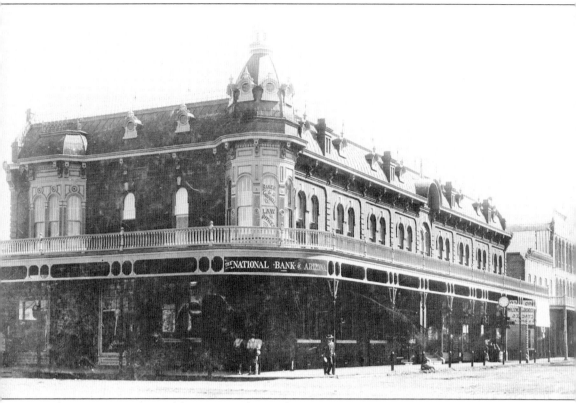

The ornate Cotton Building was at the southeast corner of Washington and Center Streets (Central Avenue) and was built around 1887. It was the home of the National Bank of Arizona, which was established in 1887 and had a capital of $100,000, surplus of $30,000, and undivided profits of $20,000, the largest numbers of the five banks in Phoenix in 1892, about the year this photograph was taken. John Yours Truly Smith, C. Goldman, Geo. W. Hoadley, M. W. Kales, and Sol Lewis were the directors at that time. The second floor had lawyers' offices, Baker and Campbell. The building was replaced by a new National Bank of Arizona construction in 1900. (Courtesy McLaughlin Collection, ASU.)

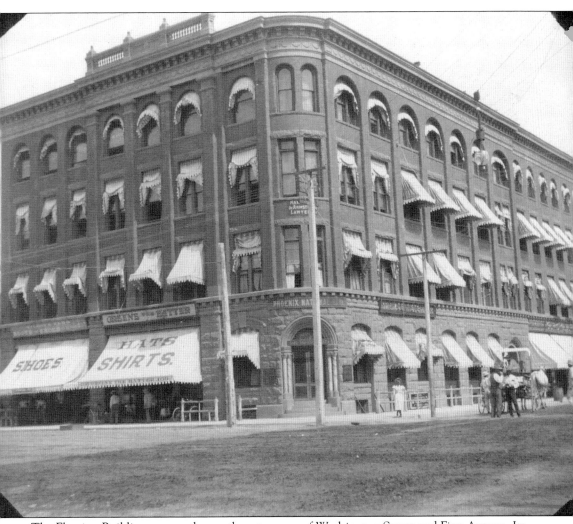

The Fleming Building was on the northwest corner of Washington Street and First Avenue. Its address was 16 North First Avenue. It was built in 1893 as a two-story building, then third and fourth floors were added in 1896. It was the long-term home of the Phoenix National Bank, with James A. Fleming being the bank's president. Fleming and his bank grew with the city because, as he said in his bank's 1892 city directory advertisement: "Special pains [are] taken to advance the agricultural, stock and mining industries, and all worthy business enterprises of the City of Phoenix, and the Territory of Arizona." The awnings on the left are for Greene the Hatter. But the building was not all business; the woman may be walking into the billiard parlour in the basement. (Courtesy McClintock Collection, Arizona Room, Phoenix Public Library.)

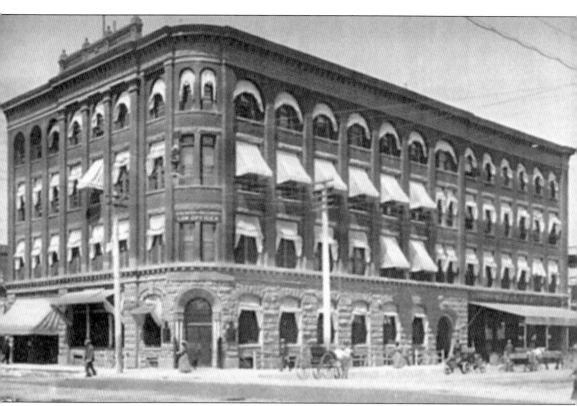

The Fleming Building was the first building in the territory of Arizona to have a passenger elevator. It was placed in service on April 27, 1896. The building is pictured here in 1905, when one of the big issues of the day was denouncing joint statehood with New Mexico. According to the 1930 city directory, many lawyers had offices upstairs, including familiar names R. M. Fennemore, J. E. Craig, H. L. Divelbess, and R. L. Jennings. The building survived until 1969 before it was torn down. (Courtesy Heberlee Collection.)

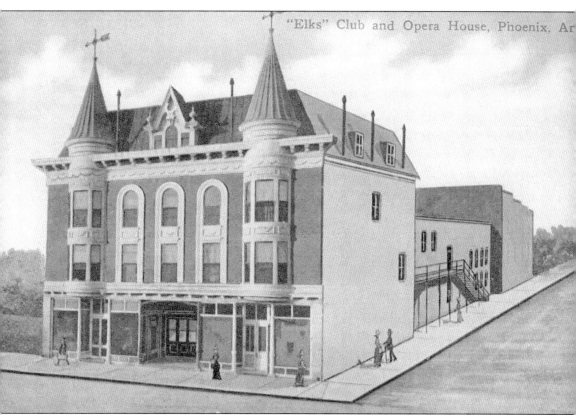

The Patton Grand Theater was located at 326 West Washington Street, and it was built in 1898. Traveling vaudeville shows, live theater, dances, and community meetings were held there, as well as opera. It was renamed the Dorris Opera House and then the Elks Club. The pretty building, with its two turrets, was the subject of early postcards like this one. This building is where one of the most important meetings in the history of Phoenix took place, when most of the land owners in the valley met and discussed solutions for their water supply. The group eventually became the Salt River Project, and the solution was the Roosevelt Dam. (Courtesy Melikian collection.)

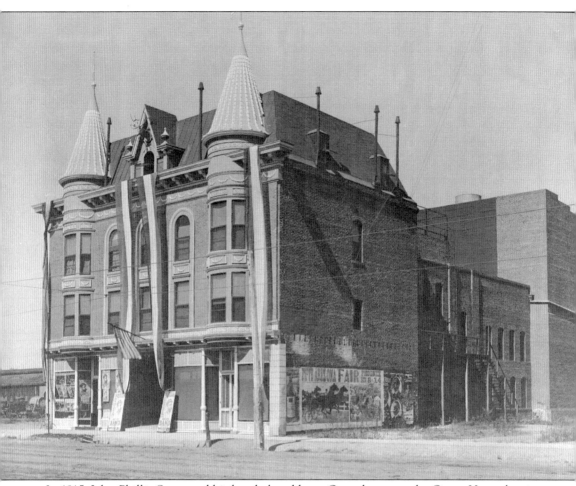

In 1915, John Phillip Sousa and his band played here. Over the years, the Opera House lost its Queen Anne-style details, but the building did survive into modern times before it was demolished around 1990 to make way for the new city municipal court building. (Courtesy McLaughlin Collection, ASU.)

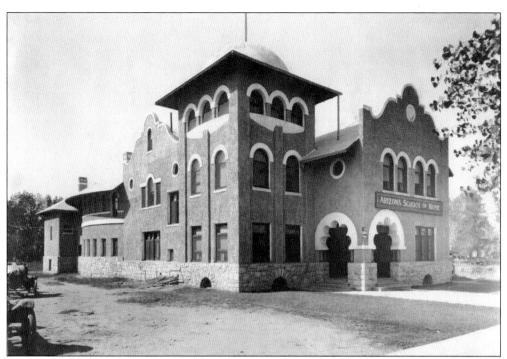

The beautiful Arizona School of Music building was located at 420 North Central Avenue and was built in 1907. Founder and director Abilena Creighton Christy and her husband, Shirley, designed the mission-style building and ran the school. It had an auditorium with a seating capacity of 600 for pupils in recital. The Christys brought international talent to Phoenix to teach music, vocals, classical dancing, elocution, and languages. The school in this building lasted until 1929. The building then became the Christian Science Reading Room, before it was torn down in the 1930s. In the bottom photograph, the sign with the swastika says, "Population Phoenix 1915 30,000. Buy Real Estate—Buy NOW. For Bargains See J. Ernest Walker." (Above, courtesy of McClintock Collection, Arizona Room, Phoenix Public Library; below, courtesy Phoenix Museum of History.)

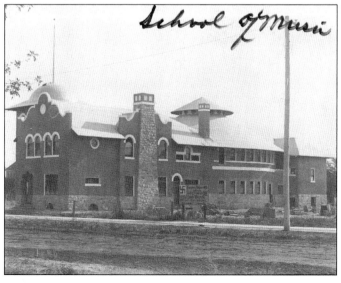

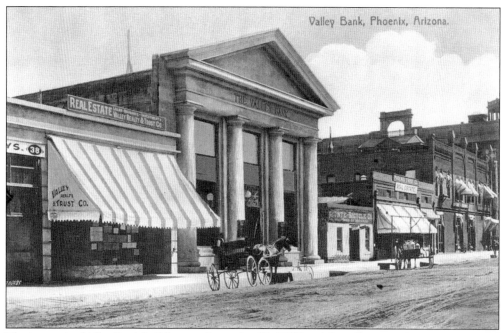

The impressive Valley Bank building was located at 28–32 West Adams Street, and it was constructed in 1908. The building was designed by architect Lee M. Fitzhugh of Fitzhugh and Fitzhugh. The bank had started in 1884 with M. H. Sherman as president and William Christy as cashier. See the horse-drawn carriage on Adams Street; it was not until 1917 that the last horse-drawn cab in the city had been replaced by an automobile. (Courtesy McLaughlin Collection, ASU.)

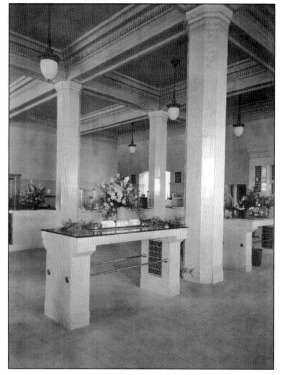

The Valley Bank building had an elegant interior, as you can see from this 1908 photograph. The 1909 Arizona Business Directory lists the bank's capital at $100,000 and its surplus and profits at $40,000. E. J. Bennitt had taken over as president when Sherman went to Los Angeles to work on their famous red car interurban trolley car system. The building's facade was altered considerably over the years, but it lasted into the 1970s. (Courtesy McClintock Collection, Arizona Room, Phoenix Public Library.)

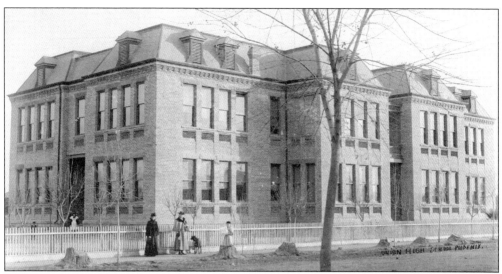

The Central School building was an 1893 expansion of an 1879 brick schoolhouse and it stood on the north side of Monroe Street, between Center Street and First Avenue. This photograph dates from the late 1890s. It had 16 classrooms to accommodate the school children in Phoenix. The building was torn down around 1920. (Courtesy McLaughlin Collection, ASU.)

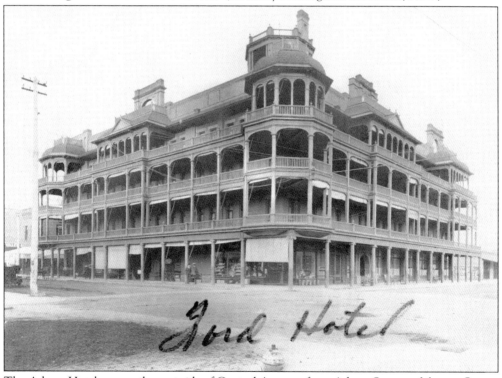

The Adams Hotel was on the east side of Central Avenue, from Adams Street to Monroe Street. It was the best accommodations in Phoenix, and for decades, it was the prominent meeting place for citizens and politicians. This original Adams Hotel was built in 1896 and burned down in a spectacular fire on May 17, 1910. The photograph is mislabeled the Ford Hotel. (Courtesy Phoenix Museum of History.)

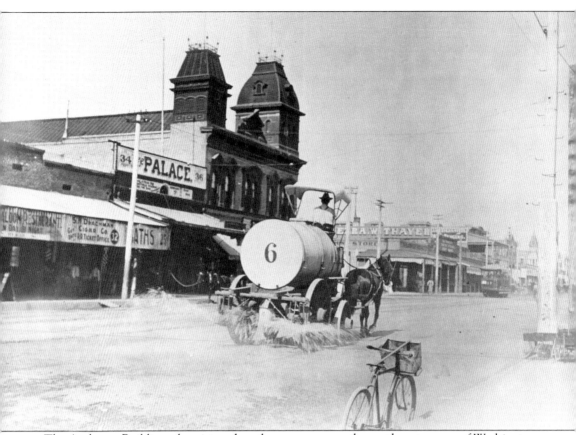

The Anderson Building, also pictured on the cover, was on the northwest corner of Washington and First Streets. The building was constructed prior to 1889. Here it is in 1900, when Washington Street was still unpaved and had to be watered occasionally to keep the dust down. The building was later called the Berryhill Building, and it had the Berryhill Office Equipment Company there at 42–48 East Washington Street. The store sold books, stationery, office supplies, Kodaks and supplies, athletic goods, victrolas, and radios in 1930. Although remodeled, the building survived into the 1980s. (Courtesy Phoenix Museum of History.)

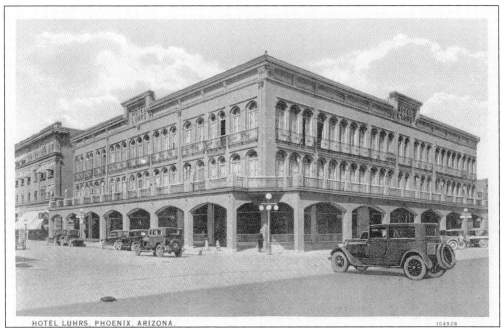

HOTEL LUHRS, PHOENIX, ARIZONA.   104926

The Commercial Hotel, later called the Luhrs Hotel, was located on the northeast corner of Central Avenue and Jefferson Street. George H. N. Luhrs built the brick hotel there in 1887, which was an important step for Phoenix's growing tourist industry. Business was great for Luhrs's Commercial Hotel, his Commercial Hotel Restaurant, and his Commercial Hotel Salon businesses, as well as the Commercial Hotel barbershop and bathrooms business, which was run by J. F. Schieck in 1892. (Courtesy Melikian collection.)

Pictured here is the lobby of the Commercial Hotel in the 1880s. The Luhrs family owned and operated the hotel until 1976. The author was lucky enough to tour the Commercial Hotel when he tried to visit George Luhrs's son, who lived in the hotel in the 1970s. The unnecessary demolition of the hotel in 1981 was the reason the author became a historic preservation advocate. (Courtesy McLaughlin Collection, ASU.)

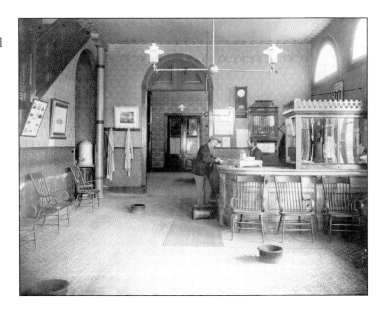

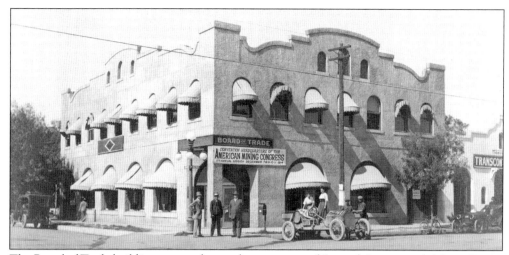

The Board of Trade building was on the northwest corner of Second Avenue and Adams Street. Phoenix business interests came together and formed the Phoenix Board of Trade in 1888 to promote boosterism. Here is a photograph of their building in 1914, when the building was probably constructed. The American Mining Congress is having their convention at the building, as the sign reads. The building was torn down in the 1950s. The car in the photograph is a reminder of the first automobile race in the state in 1908, which was staged by the *Arizona Republican* newspaper. Four cars left Los Angeles at midnight, and the winner reached Phoenix in 41.5 hours. (Courtesy Phoenix Museum of History.)

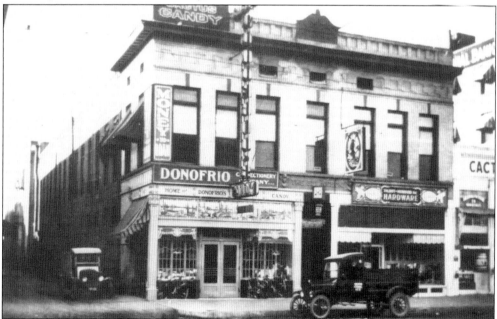

The Ellingson Building was also called the Donofrio Building because of its very popular tenant. It was at 21 West Washington Street and was built in 1899 for $40,000 by Mons Ellingson, a prominent Norwegian businessman who was a principal of the Farmers and Merchants Bank in Phoenix. There was a major effort to save this important building in the mid-1980s by current mayor Phil Gordon and then-mayor Terry Goddard by relocating it. (Courtesy Phoenix Museum of History.)

The Maricopa County Courthouse was built in 1884 at a cost of $35,000. The courthouse was located on the southwest corner of First Avenue and Washington Street, in one of two public plazas set aside in the original town site for public purposes. The Victorian structure dominated the town's skyline and served as the courthouse and county offices until it was torn down in 1928. The photograph to the right is from around 1910. (Right, courtesy Heberlee Collection; below, courtesy of McLaughlin Collection, ASU.)

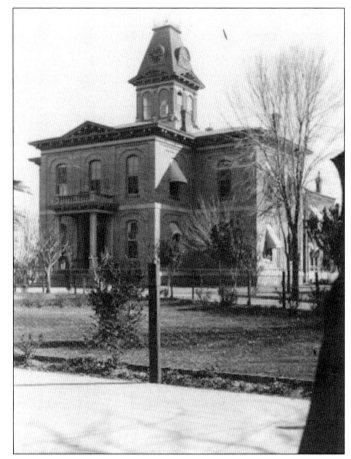

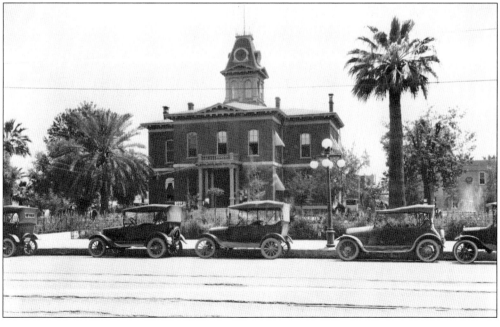

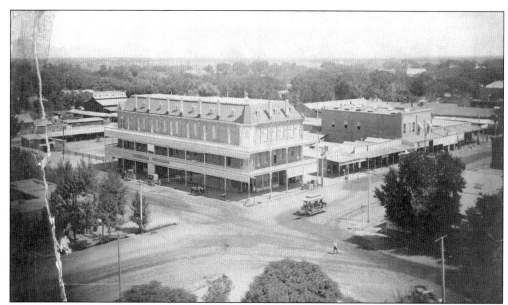

The Monihon Building was erected in 1889 and was one of Phoenix's most beautiful buildings. It was located on the northeast corner of Washington Street and First Avenue. Both photographs of it here were taken from the Maricopa County Courthouse. Note the horse-drawn trolley in the top photograph verses the electric trolley in the bottom photograph. The first photograph is before 1896 because the Adams Hotel has not been built yet behind the Monihon Building. The bottom photograph is from 1907. The great building was torn down in the mid-1930s. According to the 1950 Phoenix City Directory, "On the 17th of January, 1871, Colonel James D. Monihon, an Arizona pioneer of 1862, planted the first cottonwood tree upon the town site." (Above, courtesy Phoenix Museum of History; below, courtesy McLaughlin Collection, ASU.)

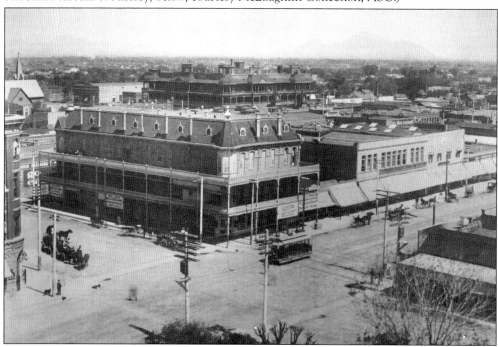

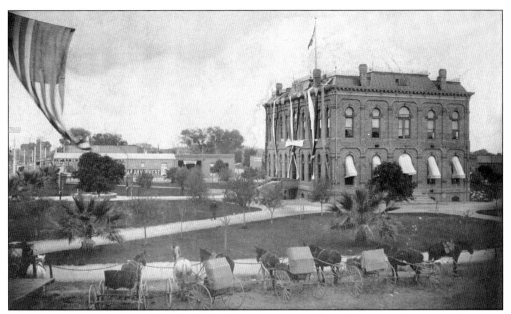

The Phoenix City Hall was on the other public square set aside in the original town site, between Washington, Jefferson, First, and Second Streets. Construction started in November 1887 by John J. Gardiner for $15,580 and was completed in 1888. When the capitol of Arizona moved from Prescott to Phoenix in 1889, this building was used as the state house, the offices of the governor and secretary, and the legislature's meeting place. They held their biennial sessions on city hall's upper floor. (Courtesy McLaughlin Collection, ASU.)

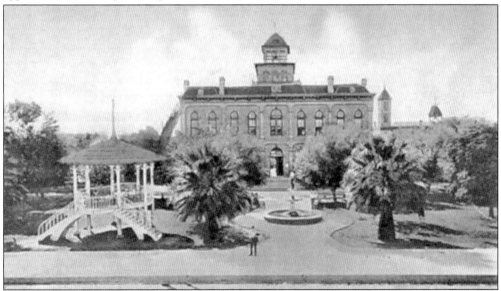

The description of the Phoenix City Hall in the 1950 Phoenix City Directory was that "the block of ground upon which the old city hall stood was known as the 'Plaza' and was originally set aside by the founders of Phoenix (in perpetuity) as a place for rest and peaceful contemplation. Their laudable desire, however was long since nullified and the ground is now used for commercial purposes." A bell tower was added in 1905. The building was torn down around 1928. (Courtesy Heberlee Collection.)

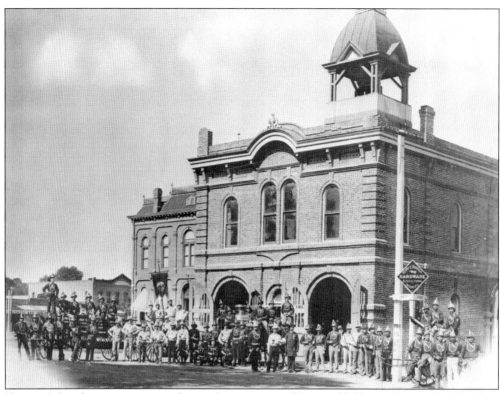

Phoenix's first fire station was on the northeast corner of First and Jefferson Streets. In 1890, fires wiped out blocks of business buildings in both Flagstaff and Prescott. Phoenix built this fire station in the early 1890s next to city hall, which is to the left of the fire station in both photographs. The photograph below shows that the building went through an extensive remodeling and added a tall tower. By 1907, there were 57 fire hydrants in Phoenix. The Phoenix Hotel is the two-story building near the bottom right hand corner of the second photograph. F. Fox was the proprietor in 1909. The building lasted into the 1970s. (Above, courtesy McLaughlin Collection, ASU; below, courtesy Phoenix Museum of History.)

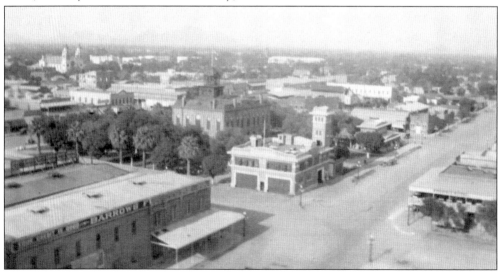

The New Mills House was built in 1893 and was at 618 West Washington Street. It was a hotel, and it replaced the Mills House, which described itself in an advertisement that it was, "Run on American plan, by Arizona Building Americans, with American labor. Running Free Bus to and from all trains. E. M. Mills, Proprietor." It became the Union Hotel by 1930 and was torn down in the 1930s. (Courtesy McLaughlin Collection, ASU.)

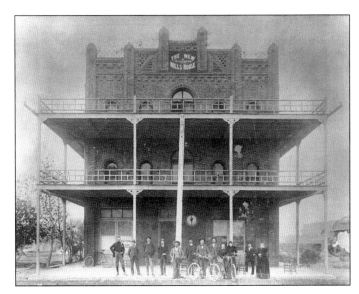

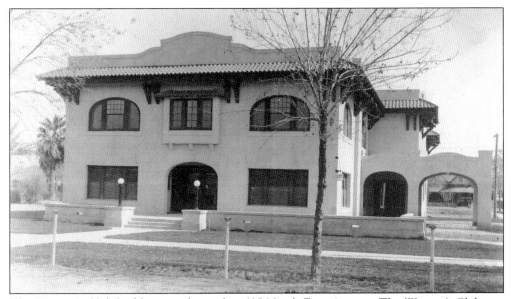

The Woman's Club building was located at 605 North First Avenue. The Woman's Club was organized in 1900 by 10 women for the "stimulation of cultural development of its members." The building was constructed in 1911 and is pictured here in 1912. An estimated 300 to 400 people came to witness the cornerstone being laid, testifying to the importance of the organization. Soon the club began to undertake Progressive reform projects for the benefit of the community. These projects included Child Study Circles, which evolved into the Parent Teachers Association; the Carnegie Free Library; public art exhibits; a juvenile court and probation system; and a "City Beautiful" clean-up campaign. In 1930, Dorris Berryhill was the president. The building was demolished soon after that for an addition to the Westward Ho Hotel. (Courtesy McClintock Collection, Arizona Room, Phoenix Public Library.)

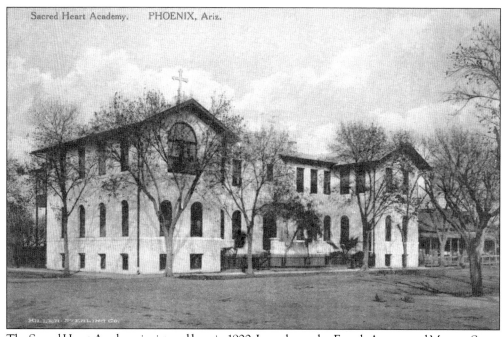

The Sacred Heart Academy is pictured here in 1900. It was located at Fourth Avenue and Monroe Street and was built in 1899. (Courtesy McClintock Collection, Arizona Room, Phoenix Public Library.)

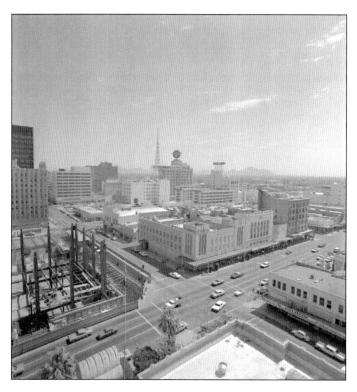

The J. J. Newberry store building on the corner in the photograph was at 36 West Washington Street, and the S. H. Kress building was to its right at 28 West Washington Street. Both stores described themselves as 5¢ to 10¢ and 25¢ stores; both opened on Washington Street, the Kress building before 1914 and J. J. Newberry around the start of the Depression; and both were successful during the Depression and afterwards. The Kress building had a detailed Moderne facade and was one of the few buildings in Phoenix executed in polychrome terra-cotta. Here they are pictured still standing in the 1970s, and they lasted past 1983. (Courtesy McLaughlin Collection, ASU.)

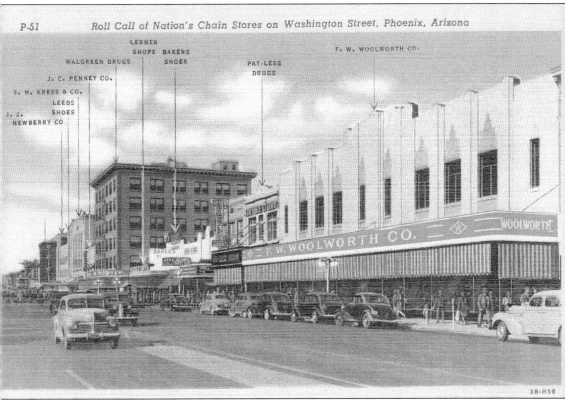

The F. W. Woolworth Company Building was at 36 East Washington Street. This is an interesting postcard because it shows downtown Phoenix when it was the shopping hub of the Valley, the "Roll Call of Nation's Chain Stores on Washington Street, Phoenix, Arizona," as the proud postcard says. It identifies no less than nine major retailers of the day that wanted to be on Washington Street in the 1950s. The art deco Woolworth building made it a special occasion to visit downtown Phoenix, and the building survived into the 1970s. (Courtesy Melikian collection.)

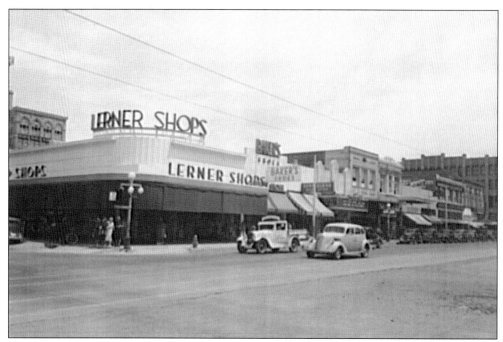

The Lerner Shops building, with its prominent sign, had a great location on the northeast corner of Washington Street and Central Avenue. It sold women's clothes at 10 East Washington Street for decades. Lerner Shops moved into the already existing building sometime around 1930, and the building lasted into the 1980s. Here it is pictured in 1940. (Courtesy Library of Congress.)

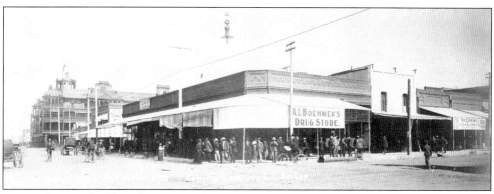

Here is the same building that Lerner Shops is in, but this photograph is much older. The date is between 1901 and 1909 because the 2-story building just to the north (left) is the Stroud Building, which was built in 1900, and the Adams Hotel burned down in 1910. The casino sign on the building on the right is not a casino but an unusual name for an insurance company, the Casino Progressive Policy Company. Phoenix voted out public gambling in 1906. (Courtesy Mclaughlin Collection, ASU.)

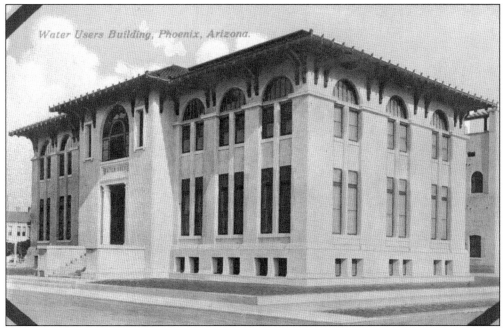

The Water Users building was on the south side of Van Buren Street, west of Central Avenue. The address was 145 West Van Buren Street. Here it is pictured in 1912, approximately when it was constructed. The building survived until 1960. (Courtesy McClintock Collection, Arizona Room, Phoenix Public Library.)

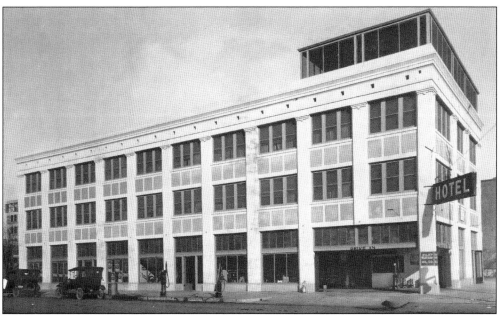

The Savoy Hotel was located at 38–40 South Second Avenue. It must have been built in the 1910s or early 1920s because the hotel looks like it catered to the automobile. It had the Wilky-Wartman Oil Company drive-in garage inside and gas pumps on the sidewalk. The building was torn down in the 1960s. (Courtesy McClintock Collection, Arizona Room, Phoenix Public Library.)

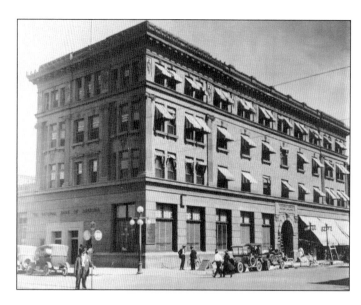

The National Bank of Arizona building replaced the Cotton Building on the southeast corner of Central Avenue and Washington Street by 1900. The address was 11 South Central Avenue. Emil Ganz was the bank's president, with $100,000 in capital and $100,000 surplus in 1909, and the bank prospered. The building lasted over 60 years and was torn down in the 1960s. (Courtesy McClintock Collection, Arizona Room, Phoenix Public Library.)

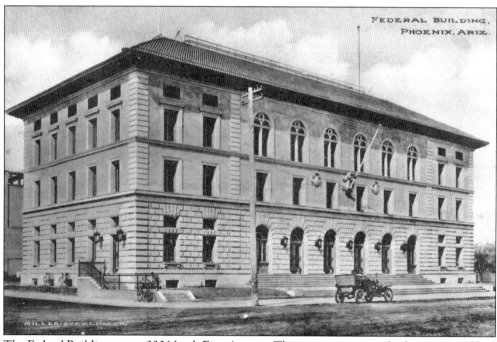

The Federal Building was at 230 North First Avenue. The construction was built in 1913 and had the post office, the U.S. District Court, and the FBI offices in the building. It was torn down in the late 1950s. (Courtesy McClintock Collection, Arizona Room, Phoenix Public Library.)

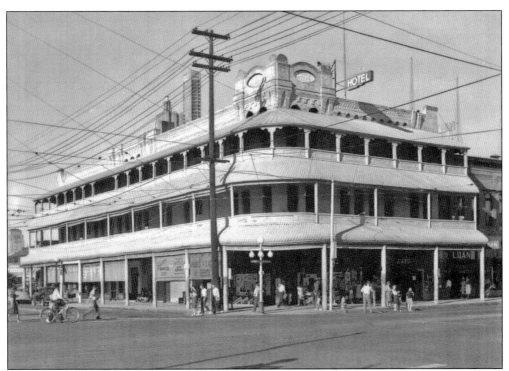

The Ford Hotel, at the northeast corner of Washington Street and Second Avenue, was built in the same year as the original Adams Hotel, 1896. The hotel was designed by prominent local architect William Norton. Its location was a little closer to the railroads, and the hotel advertised in the 1909 Arizona Business Directory as "the Popular Hotel for Commercial Men, Mining Men and Stockmen. The Traveling Public Invited." It was prominent enough that President Roosevelt spoke from the hotel's balcony at the celebration of the completion of Roosevelt Dam in 1911. The bottom photograph shows the hotel around 1940. It survived until 1969. (Above, courtesy McLaughlin Collection, ASU; below, courtesy Library of Congress.)

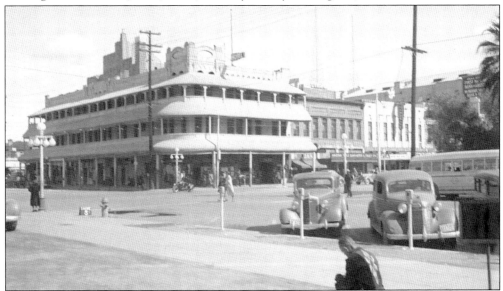

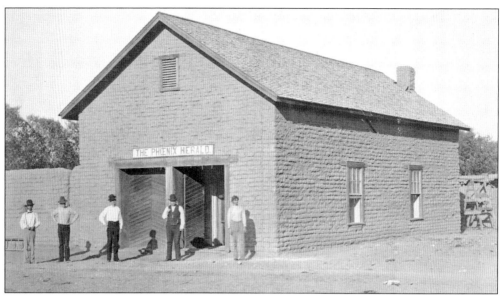

The Phoenix Herald building was one of Phoenix's very early buildings, built of adobe in the 1870s. It was reportedly located on Center Street, between Washington Street and Jefferson Street. The *Salt River Herald* was the first newspaper in Phoenix, started in 1878, and in 1879, the newspaper became the *Phoenix Herald*. It became a daily newspaper in 1881. (Courtesy McClintock Collection, Arizona Room, Phoenix Public Library.)

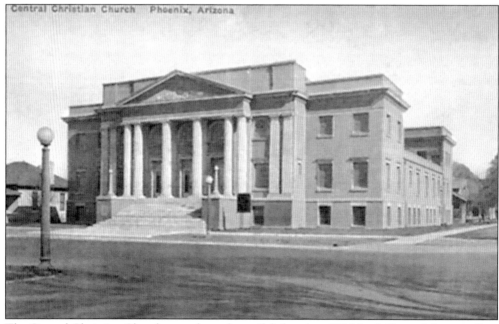

The Central Christian Church was a large, beautiful church at 801 North Central Avenue. Rev. R. E. Elmore was the pastor in 1930. The building lasted into the 1980s, at which time the author and his family tried to purchase the church to save it, but the owner had big plans for the site and demolished it, just before filing for bankruptcy. (Courtesy Heberlee Collection.)

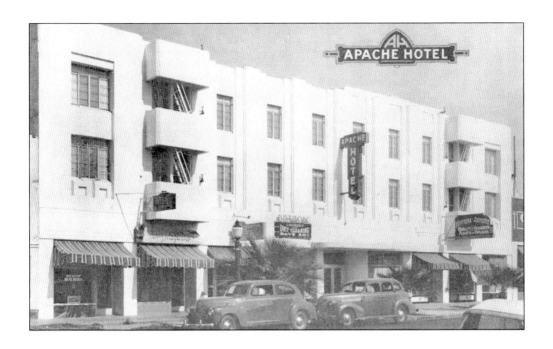

The Apache Hotel was at 509–515 North Central Avenue, with G. W. Mears as the proprietor in 1928. It described itself at that time as a "Modern Family Hotel, Dining Room in Connection." It became a second-rate hotel, being a couple of blocks too far north from the center of downtown. Here it is pictured in the 1940s and in the 1970s. It was torn down in the late 1980s. (Above, courtesy Melikian collection; below, courtesy Heberlee Collection.)

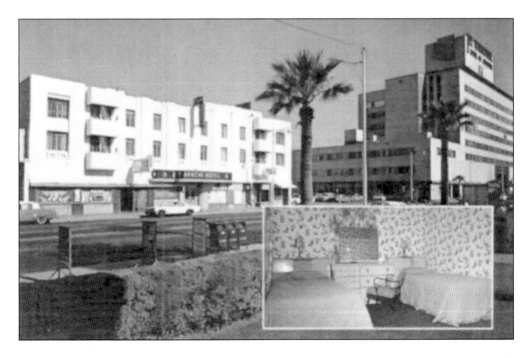

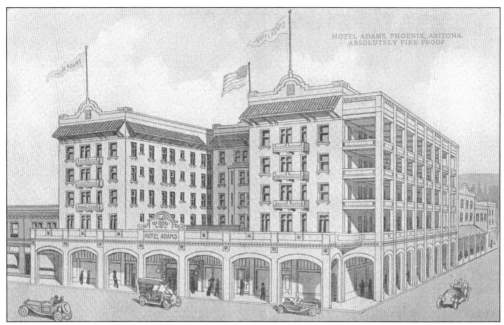

The second Adams Hotel replaced the original wooden structure after its 1910 fire. This one was absolutely fireproof, had 350 rooms, and its rates started at $2.50 in 1930. It remained the premier meeting place in downtown Phoenix, especially for politicians. The back of this postcard states, "Finest Winter Climate in the World." The building was imploded around 1974. (Courtesy Melikian collection.)

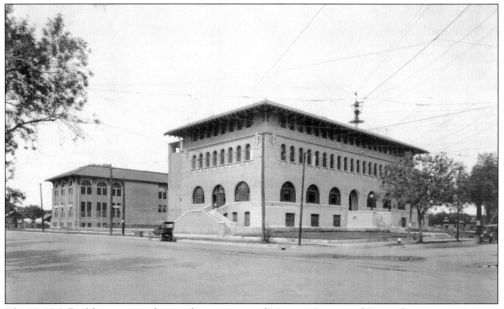

The YMCA Building was on the northeast corner of Monroe Street and Second Avenue, 140 West Monroe Street. It was constructed in 1910, and here it is pictured in 1915. It was an ambitious project considering Arizona was still a territory and the city's population was only around 11,000 people in 1910. The Water Users building is to the left of it on Van Buren Street. The building was torn down in the 1960s. (Courtesy McClintock Collection, Arizona Room, Phoenix Public Library.)

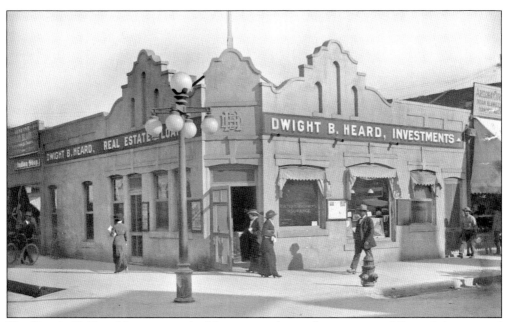

The Dwight B. Heard Investments building was at the southeast corner of Central Avenue and Adams Street. Dwight B. Heard was one of Phoenix's leading citizens, and this was his headquarters for his many real estate deals and his promotion of Phoenix. Here it is pictured in 1919, the year Heard built the tallest building in Arizona at 112 North Central Avenue. He would later finance and co-own the Hotel San Carlos. Phoenix would grow substantially, partially due to Heard's efforts, and in 1920, Phoenix would pass Tucson as the state's most populated city with 29,053 people. (Courtesy McLaughlin Collection, ASU.)

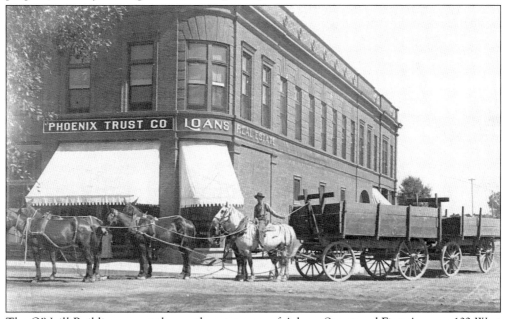

The O'Neill Building was at the northwest corner of Adams Street and First Avenue, 102 West Adams. It was constructed around 1900 and O'Neill and McKean were early Phoenix lawyers in the building. The structure was torn down around 1929. (Courtesy Phoenix Museum of History.)

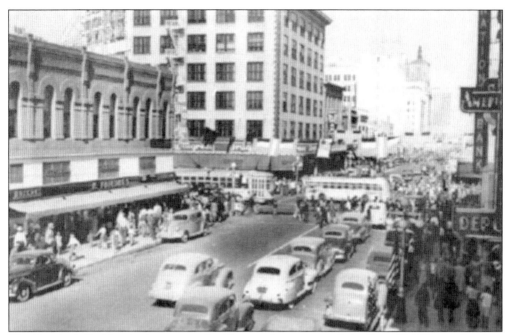

The Goodrich Building is the six-story building in the center, and the Porter Building is the two-story building on the left in this photograph from the 1940s. The photograph is looking north on Central Avenue and the buildings are on the west side of Central Avenue at Washington Street. The Goodrich Building was originally a four-story building constructed before 1900 and was expanded in the 1921 by Roy Goodrich, a well-known attorney and civic leader. Dentists and physicians were the principal tenants upstairs, and Walgreens Drugstore was the ground floor tenant for decades. The distinctive Porter Building was built before 1890. The Denver Hotel was on the second floor. Both of these buildings survived into the 1980s before being torn down. In 1925, Phoenix recorded its largest real estate transaction up to that point when a buyer paid $200,000 for a half-block in the center of the business district. (Courtesy Heberlee Collection.)

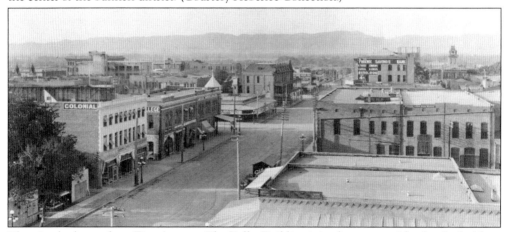

The view looks south on First Avenue. The Balke Building is in the center with what looks like a funnel on its roof. It was at the northeast corner of Adams Street and First Avenue. The address was 119 North First Avenue. The distinctive building lasted at least until 1983. The one-story building to its right is the Security Building. (Courtesy McClintock Collection, Arizona Room, Phoenix Public Library.)

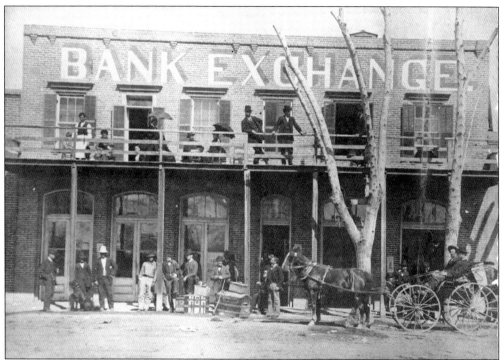

The two-story brick Bank Exchange Hotel was on the north side of Washington Street, between First and Second Street. It was Phoenix's premier hotel, owned by Mayor Emil Ganz. The hotel burned down in 1885. (Courtesy McLaughlin Collection, ASU.)

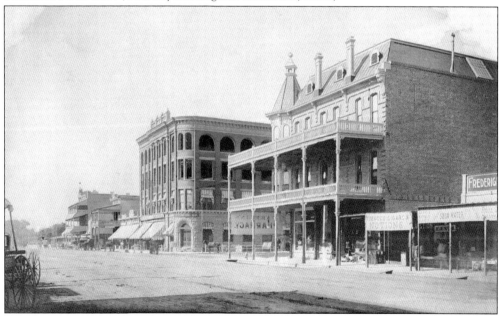

The Fleming Building and the Monihon Building are at First Avenue and Washington Street. In this photograph, the Fleming Building is completing its third and fourth floors, making the year 1896. James Monihon was the mayor of Phoenix at this time. (Courtesy McClintock Collection, Arizona Room, Phoenix Public Library.)

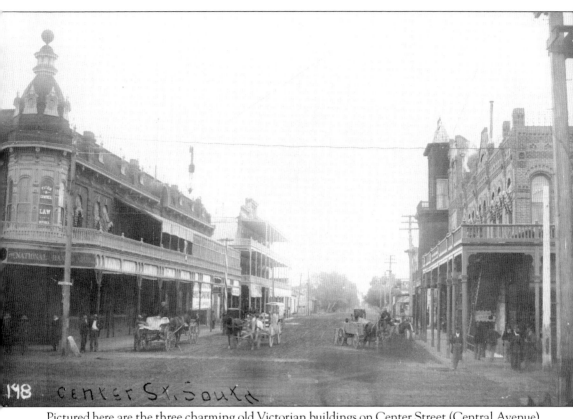

CENTER ST SOUTH

198

Pictured here are the three charming old Victorian buildings on Center Street (Central Avenue) looking south in the early 1890s. On the left is the Cotton Building, to its right is the Commercial Hotel, and across the street on the right is the Porter Building. According to a sign at the Porter Building, a shave and a hair cut cost two bits (25¢). The era of all-night saloons ended in Phoenix in 1908 as the council ordered the saloons to close at midnight and all day on Sunday. The Phoenix saloon keepers countered the ordinance by raising the price of beer to 10¢ a glass. (Courtesy McClintock Collection, Arizona Room, Phoenix Public Library.)

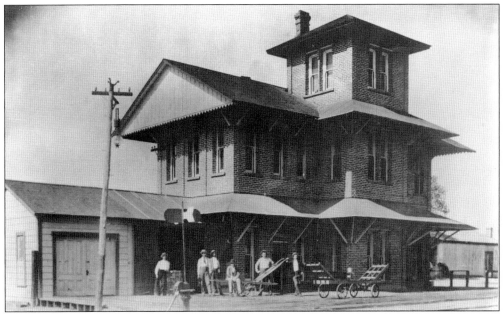

The Maricopa and Phoenix Railroad Station, nicknamed "the Blockhouse," was at the southwest corner of Seventh Street and the railroad tracks (Jackson Street). It took people between Phoenix and the city of Maricopa, some 30 miles to the south, for a connection to the Southern Pacific Railroad main line. The building was probably built soon after the arrival of the first train to Phoenix, July 4, 1887. The Southern Pacific Railroad advertisement in the 1892 Phoenix City Directory read "Quick Time and Cheap Fares To Eastern and European Cities, via the Great Trans-Continental All-Rail Routes of the Southern Pacific Co." (Courtesy McLaughlin Collection, ASU.)

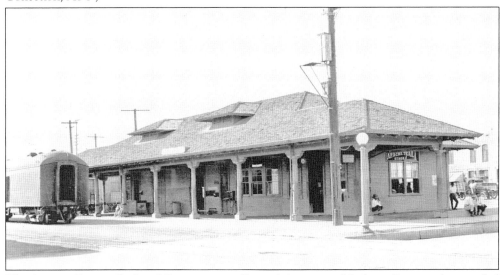

The Arizona-Eastern Railroad Station was at Central Avenue and Jackson Street and succeeded the Blockhouse. Here it is pictured in 1904. The Arizona Eastern was a subsidiary of the Southern Pacific. The decision was eventually made to unite all stations, which resulted in the building of Union Station. Union Station welcomed the first main line railroad to Phoenix in 1926, and it is still standing at Fourth Avenue and the railroad tracks. (Courtesy McLaughlin Collection, ASU.)

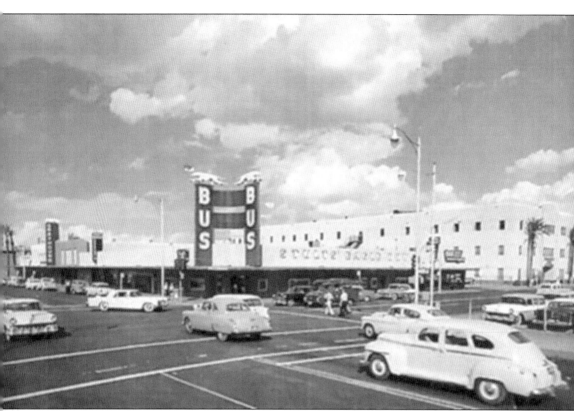

The Greyhound bus station was on the northeast corner of Van Buren and First Streets, beginning in the 1940s. Here it is pictured in the 1950s. The station had moved from its previous location at 29 East Jefferson Street. As late as 1930, all bus lines were still called stage lines in the city directory. In 1950, Phoenix had five bus lines to choose from—American Buslines, Continental Bus Lines, Las Vegas Needles Phx Stages, Pacific Greyhound Lines, and Sun Valley Bus Lines. (Courtesy Heberlee Collection.)

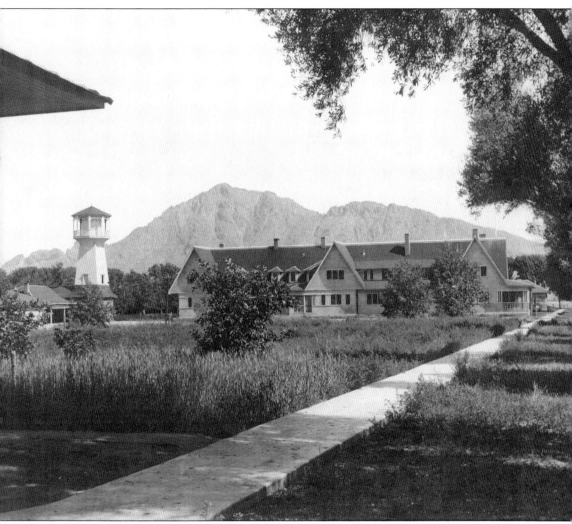

The Ingleside Club was built on East Indian School Road in 1909. As Phoenix's first winter resort, it described itself as being "Among the Orange Trees—Where Summer Loves to Linger and Winter Never Comes . . . 8 miles Northeast of Phoenix." The name changed to the Ingleside Inn, and it did not last past the 1940s. Here it is pictured in 1920 with Camelback Mountain in the background. (Courtesy McClintock Collection, Arizona Room, Phoenix Public Library.)

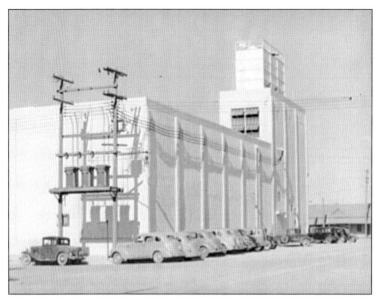

The Arizona Citrus Grower's Warehouse and Cooperative was at 601 East Jackson Street. It was an important building in the developing agriculture industry in Phoenix and was conveniently located near the railroad tracks. F. W. Avery was the manager in 1930 and R. M. Hess was the manager in 1940. (Courtesy Heberlee Collection.)

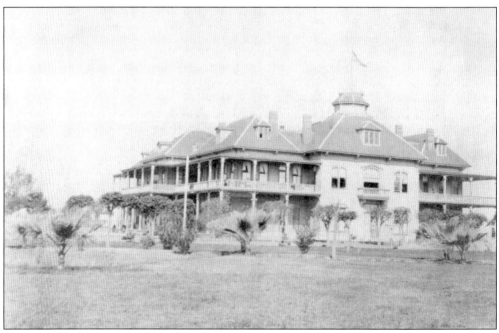

Phoenix Indian School was officially called the U.S. Indian Industrial Training (later vocational) School, and it was located at 300 East Indian School Road. Founded in 1890, this was its first building on its own campus. The building was designed by famous local architect James Creighton and was completed in 1892, the year this photograph was taken. The photographed building would become the girls dormitory. Three structures still remain from the school, but this one was torn down. The school closed in 1990. (Courtesy Phoenix Museum of History.)

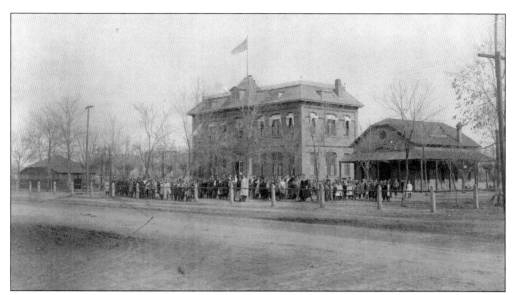

The Osborn School was on the northeast corner of Central Avenue and Osborn Road. It was built around 1892, and it was also designed by architect James Creighton. The school served children living far north of downtown, and it survived for 75 years as the city grew towards the school but was torn down in 1963. Teacher salaries were raised in 1920. Instructors in the first five grades were paid $1,125 in the first year. Teachers in upper grades were paid $1,250. (Courtesy McLaughlin Collection, ASU.)

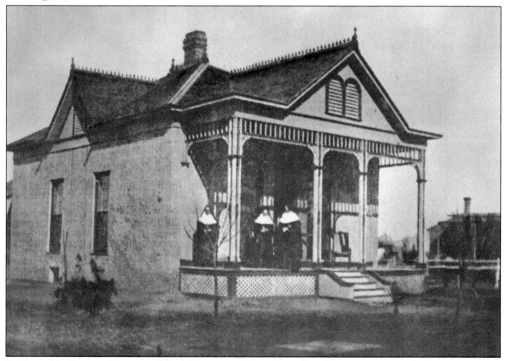

St. Joseph's Hospital's original building was at Fourth and Polk Streets. It was built in 1894 and opened in 1895. The building was Phoenix's first hospital, and it had six rooms for the Sisters of Mercy to take care of patients. (Courtesy McLaughlin Collection, ASU.)

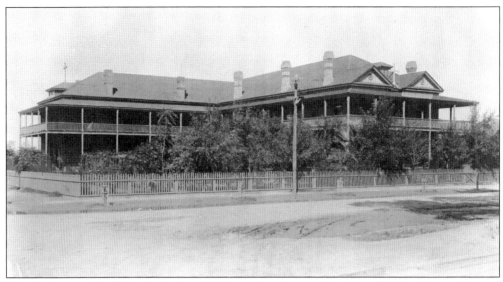

Here is the second building for St. Joseph's Hospital at the same location, 425 North Fourth Street. It was completed in 1896 (the right half of this picture), then a wing was added (the left half) in 1899. The building served until October 5, 1917, when it suffered a terrible fire. The Phoenix Union High School football team was able to get all of the patients out without any lives lost. (Courtesy McLaughlin Collection, ASU.)

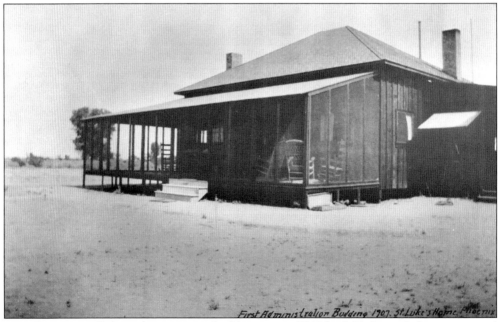

St. Luke's Hospital's first administration building was at 501 North Eighteenth Street, pictured here in 1907. The hospital started out as a sanatorium for consumptives under the supervision of Rev. J. W. Atwood. The hospital remains in the same location today. (Courtesy McLaughlin Collection, ASU.)

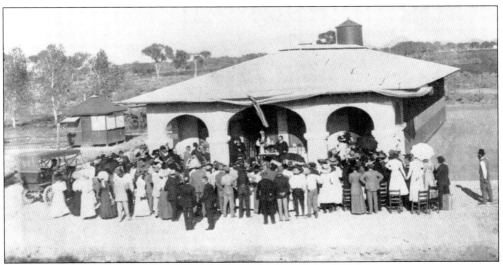

St Luke's Hospital opened its new infirmary in 1911. President Roosevelt was in town to dedicate the opening of Roosevelt Dam, so he also dedicated the infirmary, pictured here. (Courtesy McLaughlin Collection, ASU.)

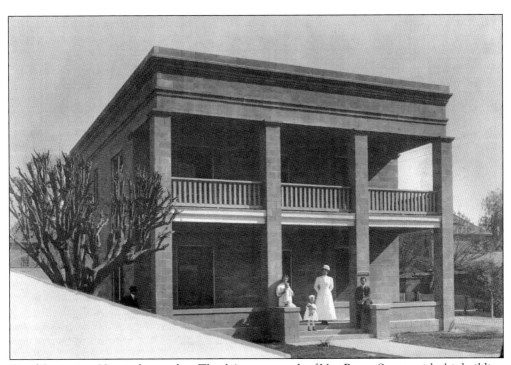

Good Samaritan Hospital started on Third Avenue, south of Van Buren Street, with this building in 1908. It was built by Dr. F. G. Angeny. By 1930, the hospital had moved to its current location on East McDowell Road. (Courtesy Mclaughlin Collection, ASU.)

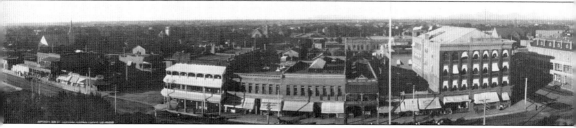

Here is a panoramic view of Phoenix in 1908 taken from the old Maricopa County Courthouse. The vanished historic buildings are, from left to right, the back of the Patton Opera House (far left), the Ford Hotel (white, three-story building), the Fleming Building (four-story building in the center), the Monihon Building (across First Avenue), the original Adams

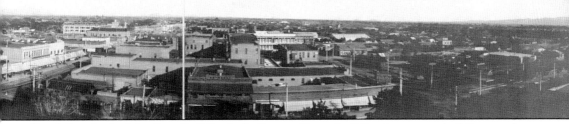

Hotel (beside the Monihon Building), the Lerner Shops building (one-story building on the corner of Central Avenue), the Anderson Building (to the right with the towers), and the Commercial Hotel (white, two-story building facing the picture in the right panel). (Courtesy McLaughlin Collection, ASU.)

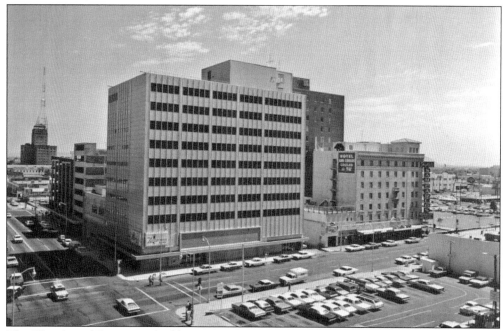

The Chamber of Commerce building was at 44 West Monroe Street. F. C. Brophy was president in the late 1940s. Originally constructed as a two-story building for the Bank of Douglas, the structure was expanded into 10 stories between 1957 and 1961. The building lasted into the first decade of the 21st century, when it was dismantled to make way for the 44 West Monroe residential condominium tower. In the 1920s, the Phoenix Chamber of Commerce sounded out possibilities of changing the name of the Salt River Valley to, "Sunny Green Spot of the West" (1920), "Happy Valley" (1920), and "Roosevelt Valley" (1925). (Courtesy McLaughlin Collection, ASU.)

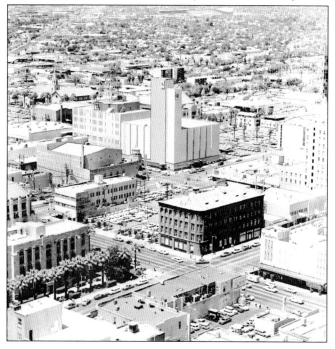

Three historic buildings lost are pictured here in 1969. They are the Ford Hotel (center left), the Fleming Building (four stories, center), and Newberry's Store (lower right). (Courtesy McLaughlin Collection, ASU.)

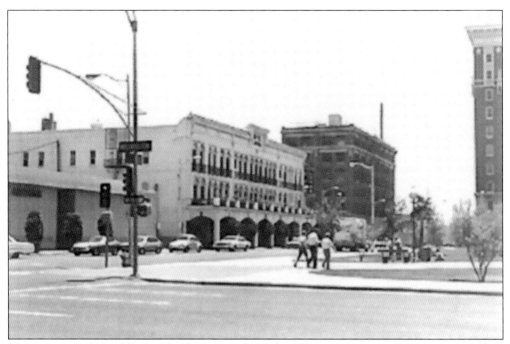

The Commercial Hotel (Luhrs Hotel) also lasted into the 1970s, as it is pictured here. It was razed by a developer who had big dreams, but the lot sat empty for 30 years. (Courtesy Heberlee Collection.)

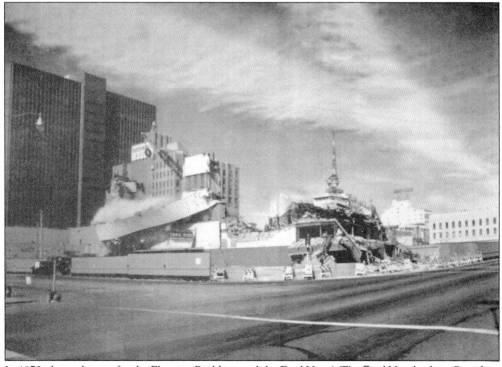

In 1970, the end came for the Fleming Building and the Ford Hotel. The Ford Hotel, where President Roosevelt had spoken from and dedicated Roosevelt Dam, is pictured here being demolished. (Courtesy McLaughlin Collection, ASU.)

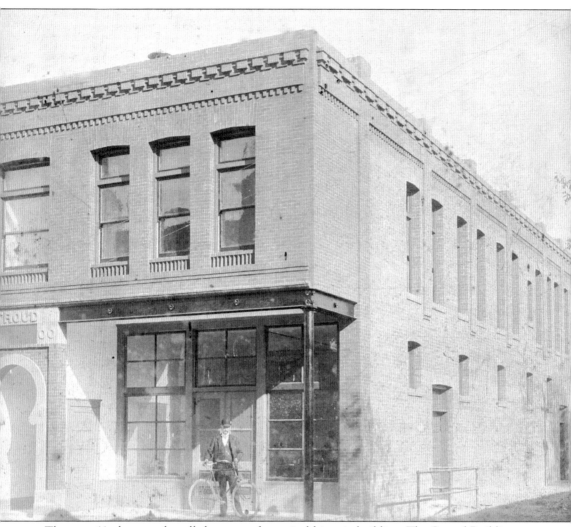

The next 11 photographs tell the story of a typical historic building. The Stroud Building was born as a beautiful two-story building with brick territorial craftsmanship and detail work, proudly built by its owner at a great location on Central Avenue in 1900. Dr. Harrison Edward Stroud was a successful doctor who had opened the Phoenix Sanatorium to treat "diseases of the chest" at 2227 North Central Avenue (where Durant's now stands) in 1895. The sanatorium helped people for nearly 50 years. In this first photograph, Dr. Stroud is posing in front of his new building. The handwritten caption, which cannot be seen here, reads, "Still standing—Dr. Harrison Stroud American Kitchen N Central 1900." (Courtesy Library of Congress.)

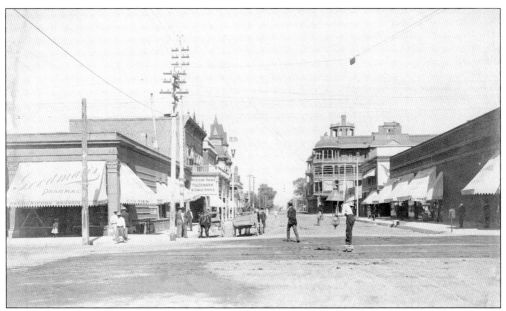

The building successfully served its purpose at 27 North Central Avenue by renting out retail spaces on the ground floor and residential rooms on the second floor. This view is looking north on Central Avenue from Washington Street between 1901 and 1910. The Stroud Building (with awnings on the second story) is located on the east (right) side of the street near the center of the block. The original Adams Hotel is seen at the right rear of the photograph. (Courtesy Library of Congress.)

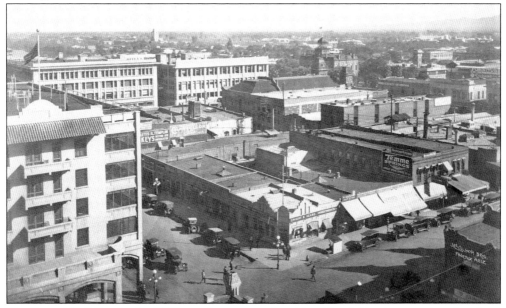

The Stroud Building in the 1920s can be seen on the right side of this photograph, taken from the Heard Building. A Temme Springs advertisement for automobile shock absorbers has been put on the north side of the building. West-facing windows on the entire block are protected from the afternoon sun by awnings. (Courtesy McClintock Collection, Arizona Room, Phoenix Public Library.)

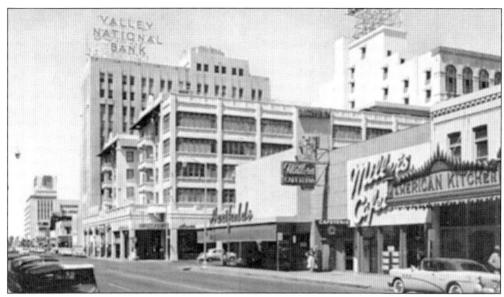

This photograph shows the Stroud Building 50 years into its life. The upper corner of the Stroud Building can be seen on the right side of this photograph. Downtown Phoenix and the building are prospering at the time. The building is completely intact, only painted, and a huge marquee has been added for the American Kitchen restaurant. The American Kitchen, one of Phoenix's famous early restaurants, had moved into 33 North Central—the retail space in the Stroud Building's northern half—right from the beginning. It was a popular community institution run by Chinese Americans. In the 1928 city directory, the restaurant is described as "Yee F. Sing, Proprietor, American and Chinese Dishes." Offices have probably replaced residential rentals on the second floor. (Courtesy Heberlee Collection.)

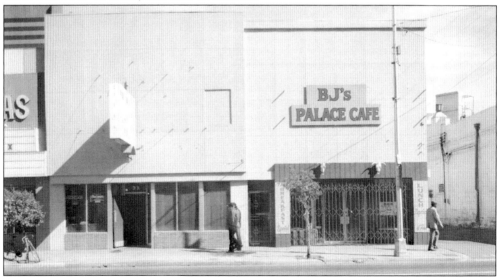

Cities change and evolve with time. In downtown Phoenix's case, Hanny's Building opened in 1947 and contributed in large part to changing the way people looked at old brick buildings. Opened after World War II, Hanny's was designed in the international style with an optimistic future in mind, and brick buildings became passé. Brick was covered, stuccoed over, or boxed in, similar to the Stroud Building as shown in this photograph. (Courtesy Library of Congress.)

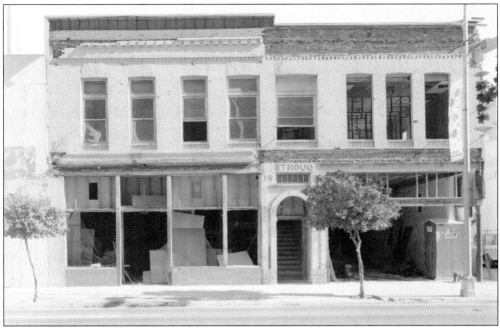

As with all historic buildings, decisions concerning maintenance, modernization, or demolition arise as the construction ages. Building owners must weigh factors such as the amount of money needed to keep the building viable, the value of the land, economic opportunities in the area, and the historic importance of the structure. For the Stroud Building, the owners chose to destroy the antiqued building. The two photographs from 1984 show that when the dismantling started, the original building was discovered to be almost completely intact underneath. The architectural details on top of the building were there, the original arched entrance was there, and even the original territorial windows survived. (Both courtesy Library of Congress.)

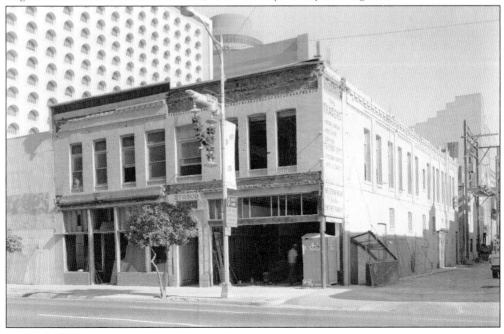

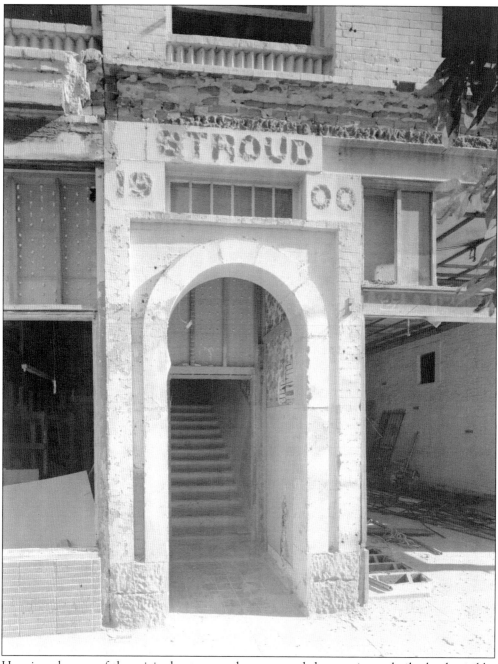

Here is a close-up of the original entrance, the name and the year it was built clearly visible, which was entombed by the 1950s facade. (Courtesy Library of Congress.)

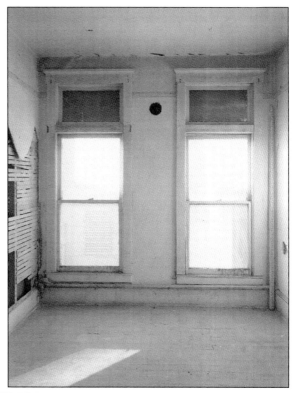

Here are photographs of the interior of the Stroud Building just before demolition. The guardrail, balusters, newel posts, and handrail, as well as the two upper-level door openings with transoms, are original features. Paneling is often put on historic building walls because of stylistic preferences and is often never removed because it is difficult and more expensive to find someone to work on the old lath and plaster walls. Ceilings are usually dropped to run ductwork above them when air conditioning is installed. The original hardwood floors remained under the linoleum floor covering. (Both courtesy Library of Congress.)

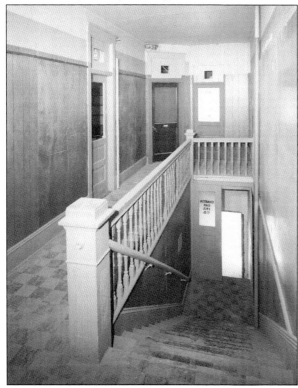

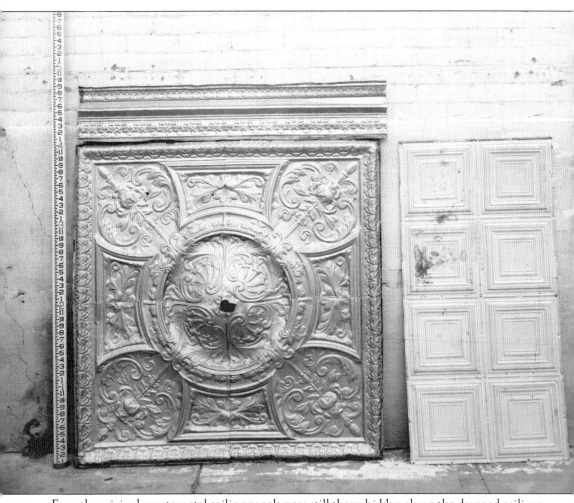

Even the original ornate metal ceiling panels were still there, hidden above the dropped ceilings. This historic building could have been saved and made back into a charming asset for downtowners to enjoy. Restauranteurs would have loved to have been on the ground floor, and great offices for the owners or others would have been an easy rental for the upstairs. It costs a lot less than you think to bypass the plumbing and electrical systems in old buildings and put in new ones. Plus the original wood timbers are much stronger than today's, and the bricks stay in fine condition if no one tinkers with them too much. The pressures to tear down buildings come from the belief that the land is worth more than the building and the unknown cost to rehabilitate it, but a successful downtown includes incentives to save historic buildings next door to new ones. The end result could have been a charming, fixed-up treasure of a building that would have been pedestrian-friendly, added soul and interest to downtown, and been patronized by more people than a new building would have been. Transferable development rights could have come into play. It is not always easy, but it is always worthwhile. History is good business and enhances every development. (Courtesy Library of Congress.)

Two

FORGOTTEN HOMES

The strength of a nation is derived from the integrity of its homes.

—Confucius

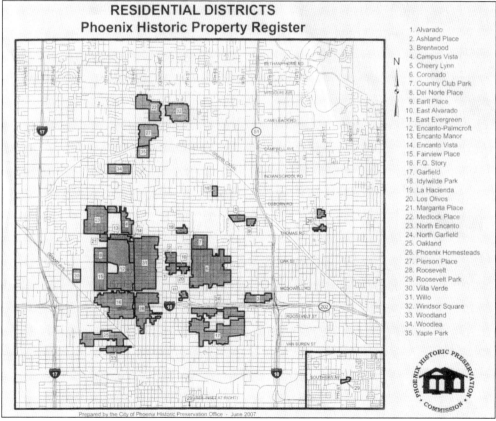

The City of Phoenix established a historic office in 1985, and the following year the first historic districts were designated. Since then, enthusiastic and dedicated homeowners in 35-central city, historic neighborhoods, have been investing time, talent, and money to preserve and restore residential architecture to its former glory. (Courtesy Phoenix Historic Neighborhoods Coalition.)

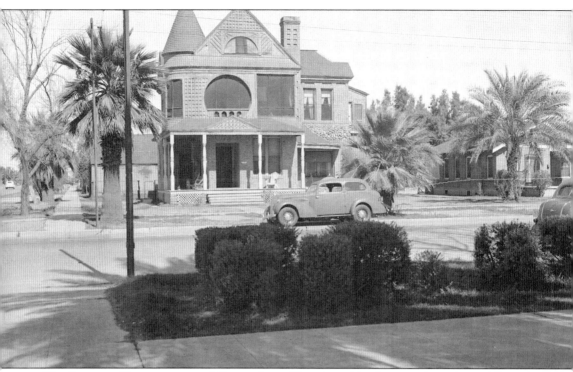

The Swetnam House, an unusual Queen Anne Victorian with a large circle in the middle and a turret, was built in 1897 and was located at the northeast corner of Adams Street and Eighteenth Avenue. Here it is pictured in 1940. Throughout the nation, including Phoenix, the advent of mass production by factories and the resulting mail order catalogs in the last decades of the 20th century meant that families of all incomes could afford to make the exterior of their homes ornate and furnish the interior through the catalogs. (Courtesy Library of Congress.)

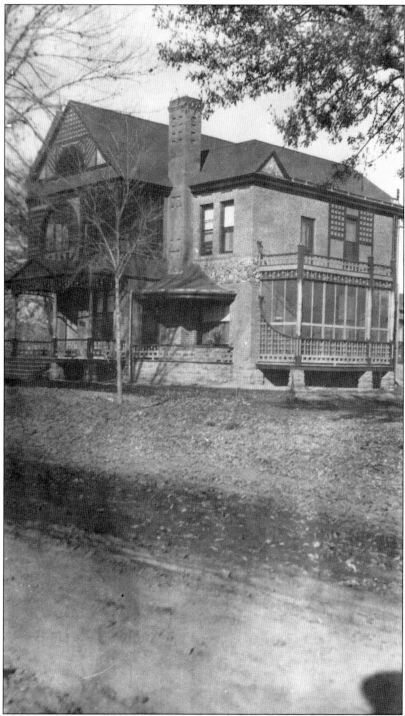

The Swetnam House is pictured here from another angle in 1920. It was built in 1897 and was still standing in 1950, but like many large old Victorians, it was probably divided up into apartments because the 1950 city directory lists three people living there with three different phone numbers. (Courtesy Phoenix Museum of History.)

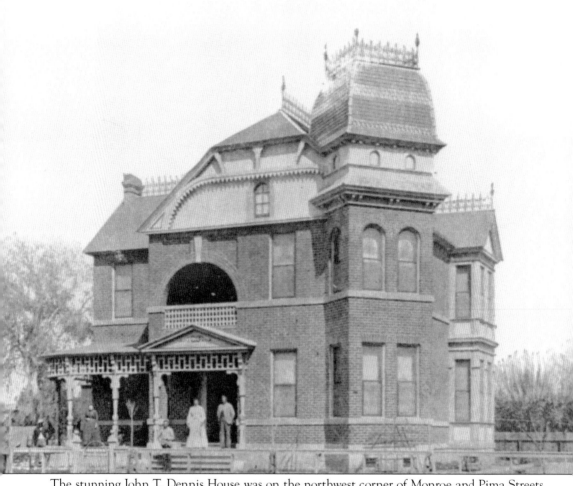

The stunning John T. Dennis House was on the northwest corner of Monroe and Pima Streets (3rd Street). East Monroe Street became the place for Phoenix's elite to build their mansions. A magnificent Queen Anne, the house was built in 1887 and torn down in 1952. The Rossen House is the only East Monroe Street mansion to survive today. (Courtesy Phoenix Museum of History.)

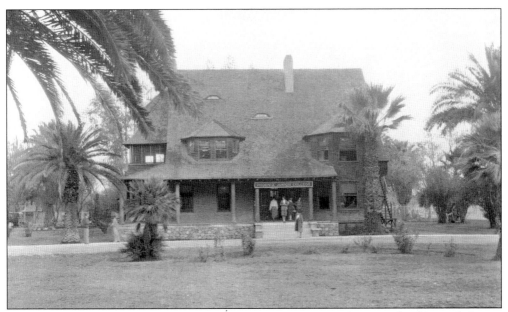

The Anderson House was at 505 North Seventh Street. It was on the east side of Seventh Street, north of Van Buren Street. The shingle-style house was probably built around 1898. It was a residence across the street from Phoenix Union High School until Phoenix Junior College was started in 1920 and took over this house as its school. This photograph is from 1926. The house was torn down in the 1930s. (Courtesy McLaughlin Collection, ASU.)

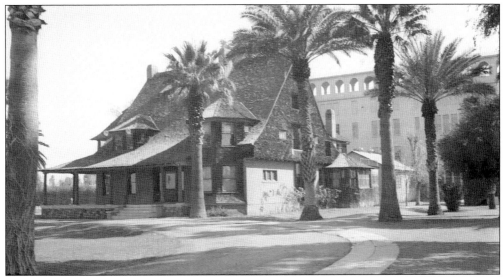

Here is another angle of the Anderson House with Phoenix Union High School's Montgomery Stadium in the background. Montgomery Stadium was a huge undertaking for the high school and for downtown Phoenix. Eighty thousand dollars had to be raised, and the stadium was dedicated on December 10, 1927. It became the envy of all Arizona school districts. Major League Baseball came to downtown Phoenix and Montgomery Stadium soon thereafter when the Chicago Cubs and Pittsburgh Pirates played a preseason game there in 1928. The stadium even hosted a national college football bowl game when the Salad Bowl was played there from 1948 to 1952. (Courtesy Library of Congress.)

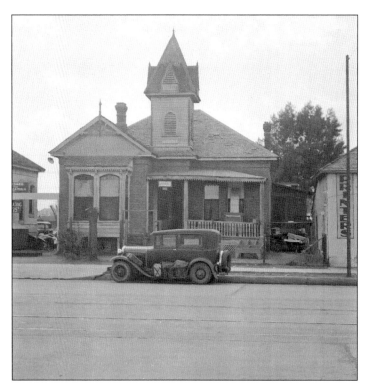

The 725 East Washington House was an unusual one with its distinctive tower in the middle. It appears to have been built in the 1890s, and by the time this picture was taken in the 1920s, Washington Street was starting to commercialize, as there is a printing business next door. The house was still standing in 1950 and must have been much larger than it looks because the building was the home of four separate people in the main house and four more in a rear apartment, according to the 1950 city directory. (Courtesy Library of Congress.)

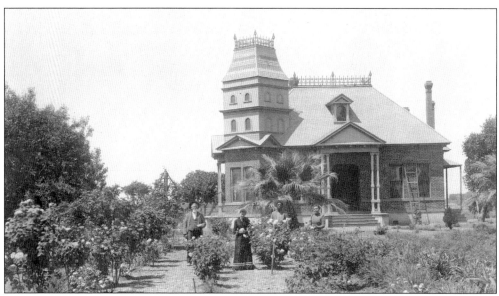

The Columbus Gray House was built in 1890 and was near Seventh and Mojave Streets. Columbus Gray was a Confederate veteran and an early Phoenix pioneer and leader. He is pictured here with his wife, Mary Adeline. (Courtesy Phoenix Museum of History.)

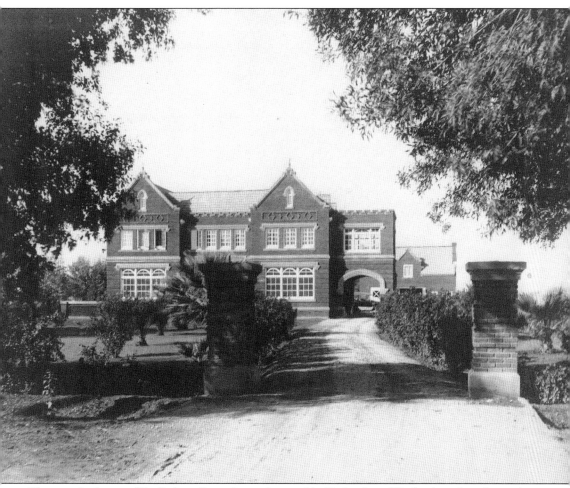

This was the house of Dr. Robert Craig. It was designed by Fitzhugh and Fitzhugh and was located at Central Avenue and Encanto Drive. The address was 727 Encanto Drive SE. An interesting story about Robert Craig was that, like many, he came here for his health in the 1890s. He lived a long life and helped people until his death in 1933. In his will, he left $150,000 to the Sisters of Mercy to help others with tuberculosis, to be payable after the death of his wife and daughter. His daughter lived until 1986. The Sisters of Mercy (St. Joseph's Hospital) received the donation then, but with 50 plus years of interest, it had grown to millions of dollars. (Courtesy Phoenix Museum of History.)

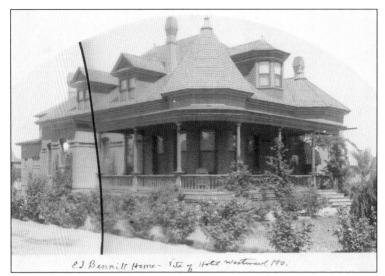

The Ephraim James Bennitt House was constructed in 1896 at 620 North Central Avenue. It lasted until the late 1920s. It was on the site of the Westward Ho Hotel. (Courtesy McClintock Collection, Arizona Room, Phoenix Public Library.)

E.J. Bennitt Home- Site of Hotel Westward Ho.

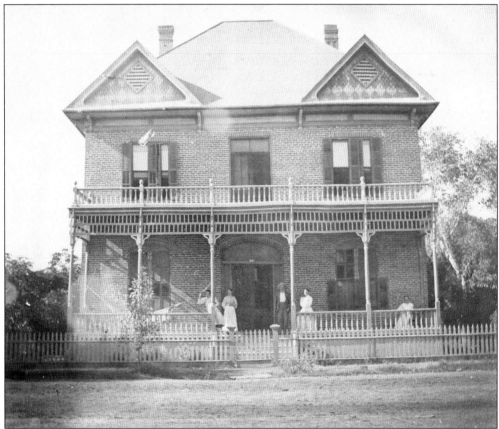

The J. Y. T Smith House was at 500 East Adams Street. John Yours Truly Smith built the house for his family in 1892. In the 1860s, Smith supplied goods to Fort McDowell and recognized the potential for hay production in the Salt River Valley. His wife, Ellen Shaver, was Phoenix's first female schoolteacher. In the 1892 city directory, he is listed as the president of the Phoenix Milling and Trading Company. The house was gone by 1928. (Courtesy Phoenix Museum of History.)

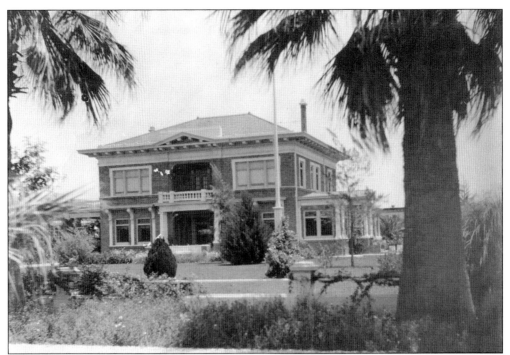

Here are two photographs of the Eisele-Diamond House, which was located at 1807 North Central Avenue. It was built in 1914 by Edward and Marie Eisele, who founded the Phoenix Bakery. Then Edward died and Marie sold the house to Issac and Nellie Diamond in 1929. The Diamonds ran the Boston Store at 201 East Washington Street. The house was torn down in 1961. The elaborate, second-floor wooden balcony railings were saved and installed on the lawn of an Encanto neighborhood home on Thirteenth Avenue. (Both courtesy McClintock Collection, Arizona Room, Phoenix Public Library.)

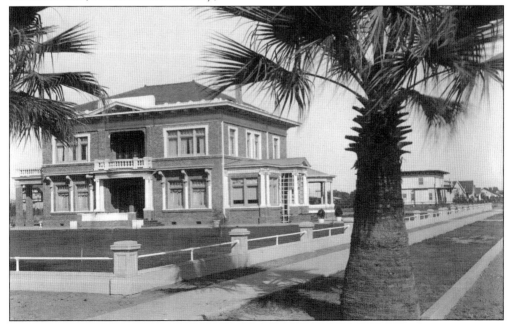

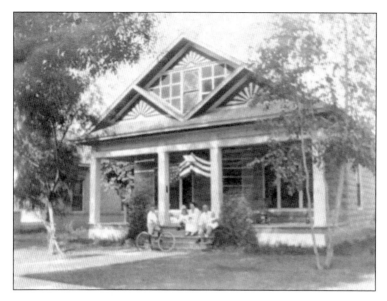

The J. W. Dawson House was at 805 North Second Street. It is pictured here in 1917. The Dawson family—Joshua; his wife, Gertrude; and his son Joshua Jr.—owned and operated the Dawson Music Company. They described their business as "Musical Instruments, Pianos, and Player Pianos, 33 and 35 West Adams" in the 1928 city directory. (Courtesy Heberlee Collection.)

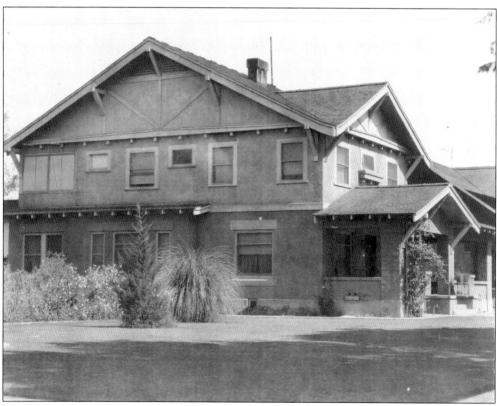

The John L. Irvin House was located at 830 North Fourth Avenue. John and his wife, Nettie, lived in this beautiful house from the 1920s to the 1940s. J. L. and O. U. Irvin ran the J. L. Irvin Realty Company. John L. Irvin's advertisement in the 1909 Arizona Business Directory reads "Buying, Selling and Exchanging Real Estate. Loaning Money and Writing Fire and Life Insurance." (Courtesy Phoenix Museum of History.)

The 3502 North Central Avenue house was far into the country, north of downtown, when it was built on the northwest corner of Mitchell Street and Central Avenue around 1900. In 1928, Alf Gregg lived here with his wife, Emma, when this picture was taken. (Courtesy Library of Congress.)

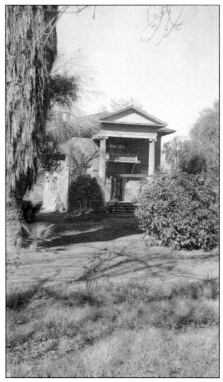

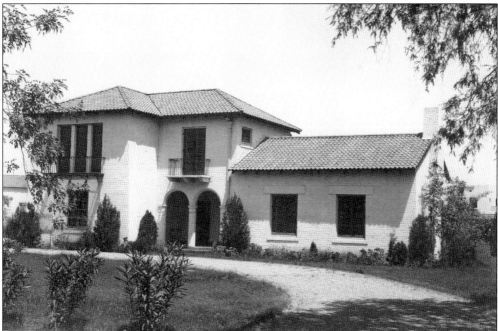

The Chalmers House was located at 230 East McDowell Road. Louis H. Chalmers, husband of Laura E., was a lawyer with Chalmers Fennemore and Nairn in 1930. He was also Dwight Heard's attorney, and he was the chairman of the board and president of the Phoenix National Bank and Phoenix Savings Bank and Trust Company. (Courtesy Phoenix Museum of History.)

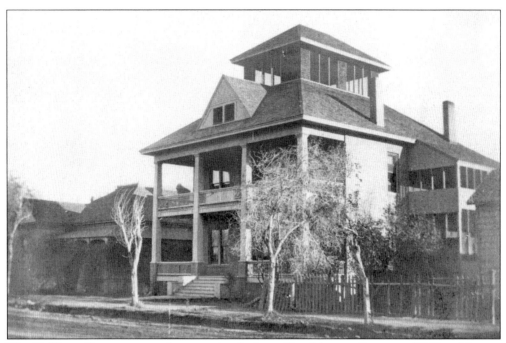

The Goldberg House was another mansion built on East Monroe Street, at 510 East Monroe Street. It is likely the house was built before 1892 because Aaron Goldberg is listed in the 1892 Phoenix City Directory as "A. Goldberg (Goldberg Brothers.) res Monroe bet Pima and Maricopa." (Courtesy Phoenix Museum of History.)

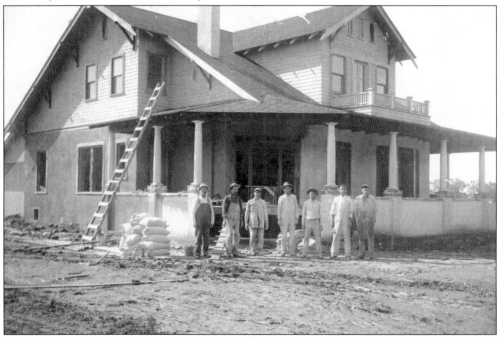

The H. C. Yeager House was in the final stages of construction when it was pictured here in 1920. Note the beautifully columned wrap-around porch. Harry Yeager, teacher, lived at 1112 North Third Street in 1928. (Courtesy Phoenix Museum of History.)

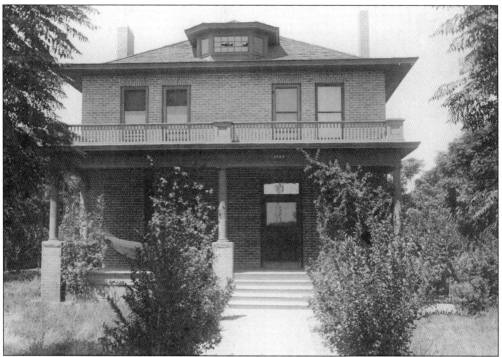

The Lloyd Christy House was at 1048 North Central Avenue (later 1026 North Central Avenue). Christy began as a clerk for the Valley Bank and had worked his way to manager when this photograph was taken in 1905. He later became mayor of Phoenix. The home was still standing as late as 1950. (Courtesy McClintock Collection, Arizona Room, Phoenix Public Library.)

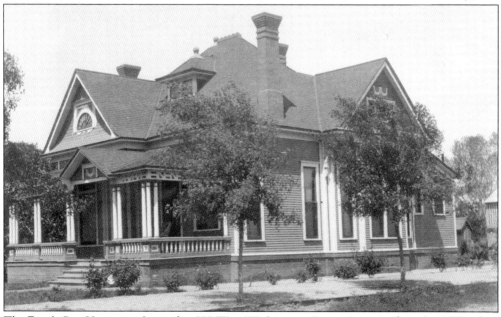

The Frank Cox House was located at 802 West Washington Street. It was built in the 1890s when Frank Cox was the district attorney and a partner with the firm Cox, Street, and Williams. The house was gone by 1928. (Courtesy McClintock Collection, Arizona Room, Phoenix Public Library.)

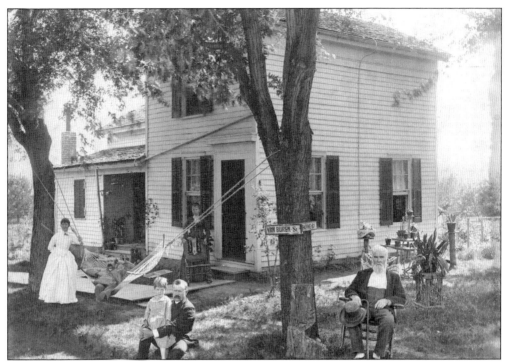

The Stinson House was a very early Phoenix home at Fourth and Van Buren Streets in 1879. (Courtesy Phoenix Museum of History.)

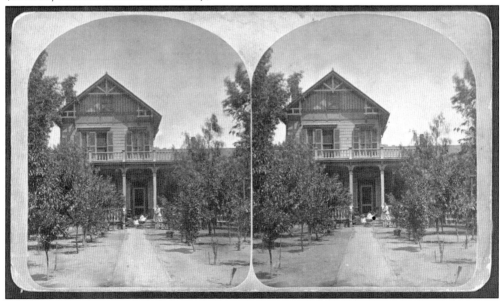

This first Churchill House was at 208 East Monroe Street. It was the home Clark Churchill and his wife lived in before and during the construction of their mansion on Van Buren. Due to financial difficulties, he sold his Van Buren mansion for Phoenix Union High School and never lived in it. Clark Churchill is listed in the 1892 city directory as "Lawyer and propr Churchill's Addition to Phoenix, res Monroe cor Maricopa." The house lasted into the 1930s. (Courtesy Phoenix Museum of History.)

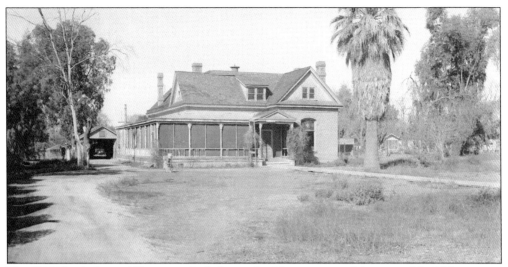

The 3320 North Central House was built far north of the city around the turn of the 20th century. It was just south of Osborn, and the Osborn School was one of the few buildings in the area. The house still had a great deal of room around it, as this photograph around 1933 shows. The house survived into the 1940s. (Courtesy Library of Congress.)

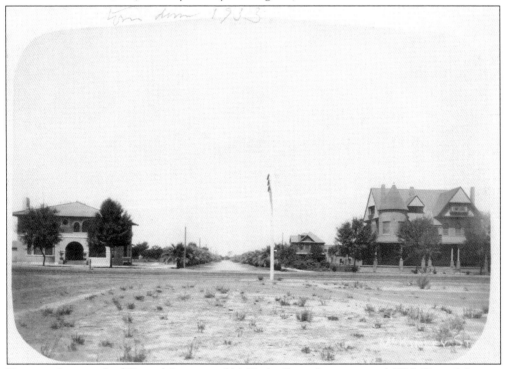

Here is a photograph of Central Avenue and McKinley Street homes around 1900. Central Avenue runs right and left, and the photograph faces east on McKinley Street. The Queen Anne house on the right was the residence of W. S. Pickrell, a prominent ostrich farmer. The usual patterns with new subdivisions at that time were that larger homes were built first and on the corners to attract interest. Around this time, the mansions of Phoenix started to move north from downtown. (Courtesy McClintock Collection, Arizona Room, Phoenix Public Library.)

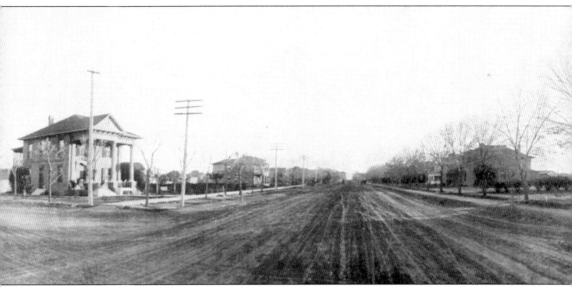

Here is a view of the same two homes shown in the previous photograph but now facing north on of Central Avenue, which is visible on the left. Central Avenue home lots began to sell in earnest

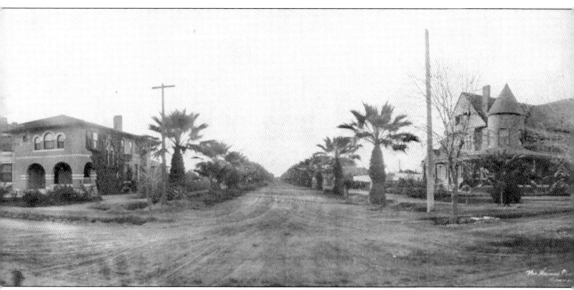

and filled in slowly. Looking at the height of the palm trees and the addition of more electric poles, a little time has passed since the first photograph. (Courtesy Phoenix Museum of History.)

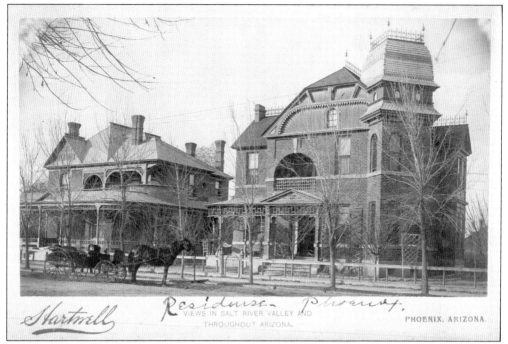

Here are views of what the mansions on East Monroe Street looked like. This is the Jacobs House on the left and the J. T. Dennis House on the right in both photographs, built between Second and Third Streets. The top photograph was taken in the 1890s when the homes were built. The bottom photograph shows that the homes survived into the 1950s. The Jacobs House even lasted into the 1960s. Imagine what a draw these homes would have been in the downtown area today if they survived and the Herberger Theater was put elsewhere. (Above, courtesy McLaughlin Collection, ASU; below, courtesy Phoenix Museum of History.)

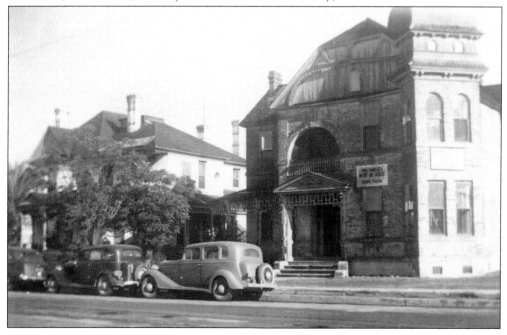

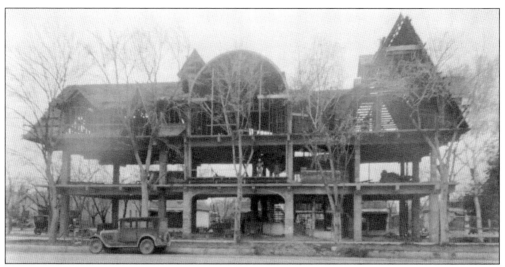

The Hattie Mosher House was on the east side of Central Avenue, just north of Van Buren Street. Hattie was the daughter of prominent Phoenix businessman William Lount, the family that was in the ice-making and delivery business. An entire book could be written about Mosher's decades-long battle with the City of Phoenix. Armed with plenty of money, she started building this behemoth in the second decade of the 20th century and spent the balance of her fortune and life litigating with the city over her rights. This shell of a house sat empty and graced Central Avenue until at least 1929. (Courtesy McLaughlin Collection, ASU.)

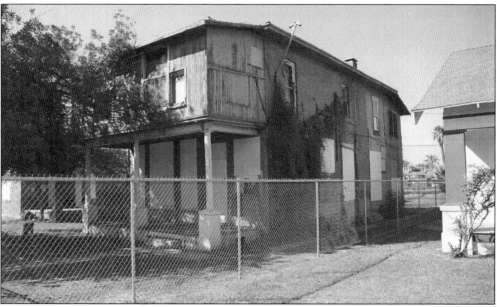

Here are two recent examples of lost opportunities. The Frank Asher House was at 620 North Fifth Street. It was built in 1910 and had all of its original features intact, including beautifully crafted built-in woodwork that was unpainted for almost 100 years. The city, instead of encouraging a pedestrian friendly opportunist to take the house, decided that a mid-rise office building would be a better use for the area. The government did provide the opportunity for the house to be moved, but its height provided too great a challenge. The city razed the structure in 2006. (Courtesy Melikian collection.)

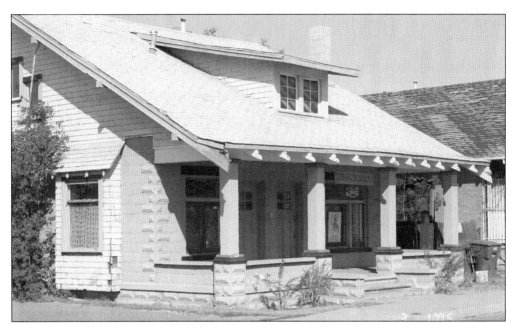

Here is the Wright House, a historic home on Seventh Street north of McKinley Street, another example of a lost opportunity, but this time in private hands. It was built in 1912 and was a first in several construction categories. It was a beautifully intact home that survived almost 100 years, until 2007. The friendly owner wanted more space on the lot and did not appreciate the history of the home. They gave the community an opportunity to move the house, but it was not feasible. With no incentive in the owner's mind to save the historic building and no prohibition from demolishing it, the owner razed the structure. (Both courtesy Melikian collection.)

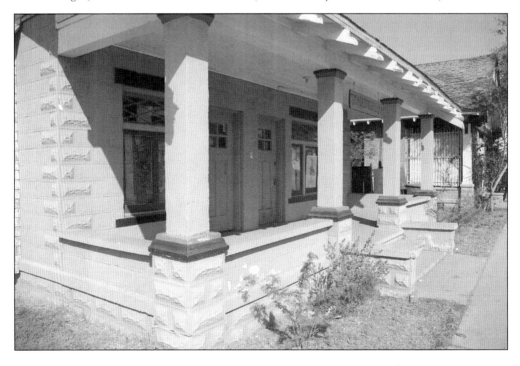

Three

Wonderful Past Businesses and Places

*Don't it always seem to go / That you don't know what you've got 'til
it's gone / They paved paradise and put up a parking lot.*
—Joni Mitchell, "Big Yellow Taxi"

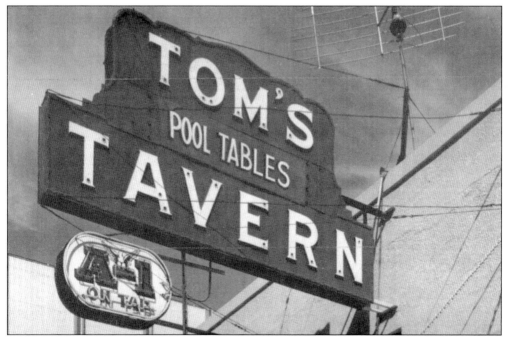

This chapter includes interesting places from the city's past, places like Tom's Tavern, a popular downtown establishment for eating, drinking, and playing pool, especially during lunch hour. It was located at 136 West Adams Street across the street from the Orpheum Theatre, now the parking lot for the Transamerica Title building. Tom's Tavern started way back in 1931 and became the Tavern Café and Billiard Parlor from 1938 to 1940. Jos A. Loges took over the existing Tavern Café and Billiard Parlor in 1941 and turned it back into Tom's Tavern. He expanded the business into 138 West Adams Street for his Tavern Liquor Store in 1949. The business lasted until 1976. A restaurant on Washington Street uses the name today. (Courtesy Melikian collection.)

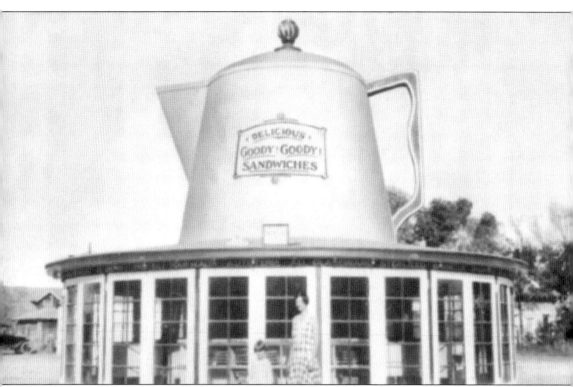

Phoenix had its share of whimsical buildings. The Coffee Pot was at 1601 North Seventh Street, the northeast corner of Seventh Street and McDowell Road. The restaurant was started in 1931, when it was pictured here, during the Depression selling low-cost coffee and sandwiches. On the brim of the saucer, it reads "PROTECT YOUR HEALTH," "AUTOTERIA," and "ALL GLASSWARE STERILIZED." J. J. Bacon was the manager in 1940. (Courtesy Heberlee Collection.)

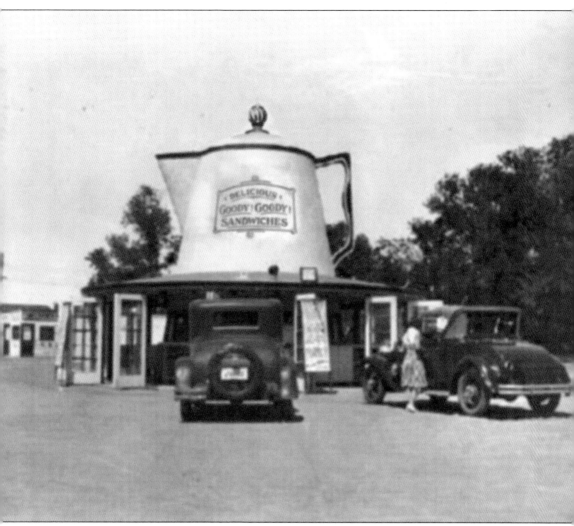

The Coffee Pot's menu in this photograph can be read to offer, for 20¢, a beef sandwich, ham sandwich, or tuna fish. A hamburger cost 15¢. The establishment had became Bennitt's Coffee Pot by 1950, owned by George Bennett. The building was ahead of its time with a wall of doors that could completely open. The coffee continued to be poured into the 1950s. (Courtesy Heberlee Collection.)

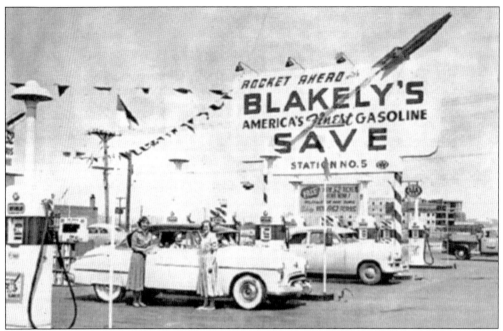

Blakely's Self Service Stations were a big part of growing up in Phoenix in the 1950s. A. Monroe Blakely, husband to Dorothy, started them in the late 1940s and by 1950 had seven locations: 702 West Thomas Road (above), 1829 West Buckeye Road, 2926 East Indian School Road, 1302 Grand Avenue, 3701 North Central Avenue, 102 East Madison Street, and 1830 East McDowell Road. You can see St. Joseph's Hospital being built in the background of the top photograph. The rocket was their trademark and easily identified the stations. The glasses given out with southwest designs are now collectors items. (Both courtesy Heberlee Collection.)

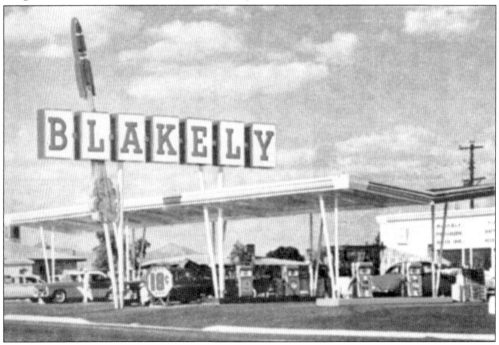

Pictured here are the Cactus street lights. The City of Phoenix installed streetlights made to look like cacti to the delight of residents and tourists. Here is one pictured on Central Avenue across the street from the Westward Ho Hotel. (Courtesy Library of Congress.)

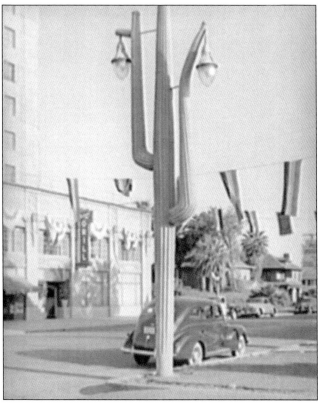

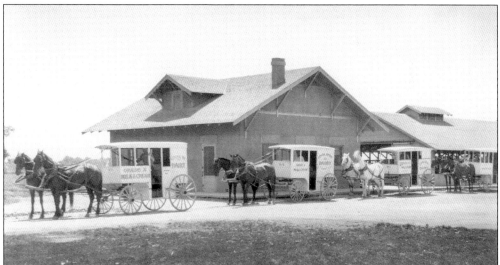

The Central Avenue Dairy was once located where Park Central is today. It was at 3104 North Central Avenue. The Geare family owned and ran it: Thos C. was president, Edwin A. was vice president, Jas F. was secretary, and Hubert E. was treasurer and general manager in 1930. Here the dairy is photographed in 1937 with delivery wagons, a familiar sight on Phoenix streets. The Geare family proudly advertised as "Arizona's Finest Dairy Products." By 1950, it was listed under the name of Carnation Company, and the property was developed into Park Central Mall in the mid-1950s. (Courtesy McLaughlin Collection, ASU.)

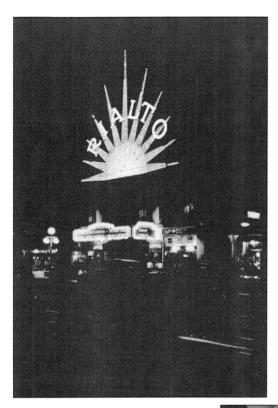

The Rialto Theatre was at 37 West Washington Street, and L. P. Weaver was the manager in 1930. Phoenix had many theatres and movie houses downtown for people to enjoy live theater, burlesque, motion pictures, and traveling shows. At the time, *The Idle Class* with Charlie Chaplin was playing, and soon after, *Mama's Affairs* starring Connie Talmadge would be playing. Connie Talmadge was the blonde sister, and her sister Norma Talmadge was the brunette. The movies make the year of this photograph 1921. (Courtesy McLaughlin Collection, ASU.)

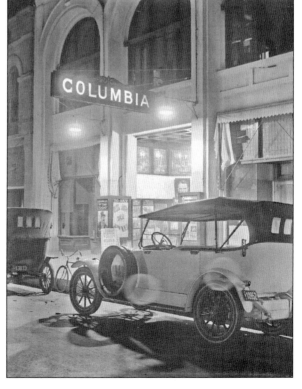

The Columbia was on the north side of Adams Street between First and Second Avenues, 110 West Adams Street. It had stained glass windows in its entryway. In the photograph, it is advertising the silent motion pictures *Ramona* and *Polly Ann*, which make the year 1917. (Courtesy McLaughlin Collection, ASU.)

The Lamara Theatre played Paramount pictures. It is advertising William S. Hart in *The Narrow Trail*, released in 1917. The Lamara started in 1915 and was located at 13 West Washington Street. It is hard to see the movie ticket prices in this photograph, but they were as follows: children—5¢, adults—15¢, and reserved—25¢. (Courtesy McLaughlin Collection, ASU.)

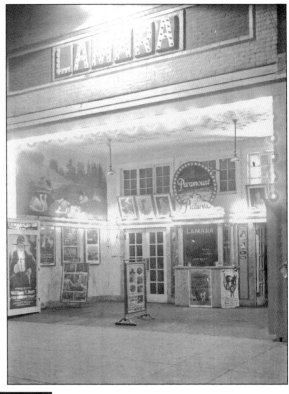

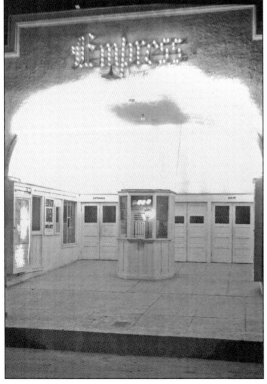

The Empress, like the Columbia and the Lamara, did not survive to 1930. The Empress first appeared in the 1913 Phoenix City Directory at 40 East Adams Street. When it opened, there were five other theaters in Phoenix: the Coliseum on First Street at the corner of Monroe Street (it was Phoenix's only movie house around 1919, a big tin building with benches for seats); the Elks Theatre at 332 West Washington Street; the Savoy Theatre on Adams Street at the corner of First Street; the Third Avenue Theatre on South Third Avenue between Washington and Jefferson Streets; and the Wigwam Theatre at 31 North First Avenue. Other Phoenix theaters now lost are the Amuzu Theatre, 210 East Washington Street; the Plaza Theatre, 132 East Washington Street; the Ramona Theatre, 313 East Washington Street; and the Strand Theatre, 116 West Washington Street. Since the 1920s, the Orpheum Theatre is the only downtown theatre still in existence. (Courtesy of McLaughlin Collection, ASU.)

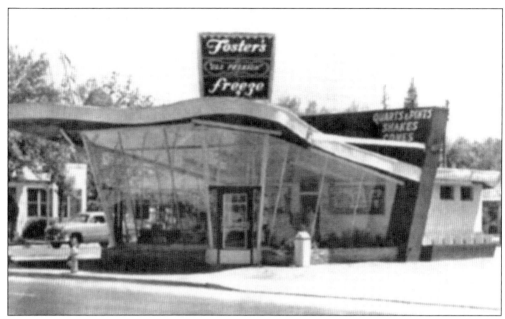

Foster's Freeze was at Twelfth Street and McDowell Road, near Good Samaritan Hospital. Here it is pictured in 1951. East McDowell Road would be called "the miracle mile" as an advertising promotion by local merchants that was meant to draw business to their restaurants and retail shops. (Courtesy Heberlee Collection.)

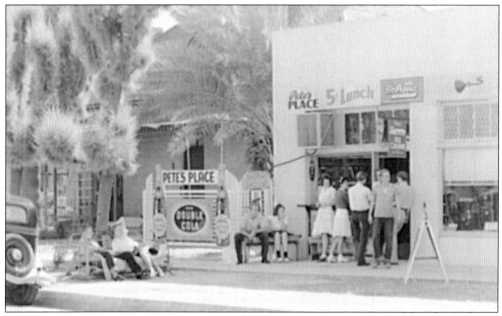

Pete's Place was one of many small eating and ice cream places around Phoenix Union High School where the students gathered. One could get a lunch for 5¢, like the sign says. Here it is pictured in 1940. Other establishments were the Igloo Lunch Stand, 409 North Seventh Street; the Campus Den, 307 North Seventh Street; the Dew Drop Inn, 311 North Seventh Street; McGee's Sandwich and Malt Shop, 625 East Van Buren Street; and Carl's Café, 637 East Van Buren Street. (Courtesy Library of Congress.)

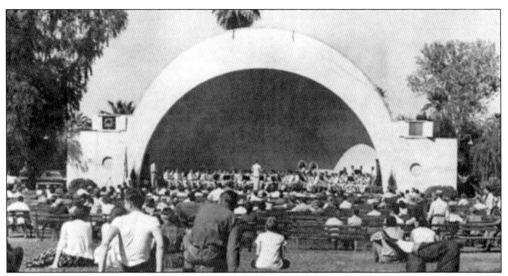

The Encanto Park band shell was part of the enchantment of Encanto Park. Classical orchestras, rock and roll bands, and school bands all played there. It was a gathering spot for the neighborhoods, church groups, and political events. The band shell survived until 2000. It was lost in an arson fire that occurred one day after a historic researcher called the city and asked questions about it. (Courtesy Heberlee Collection.)

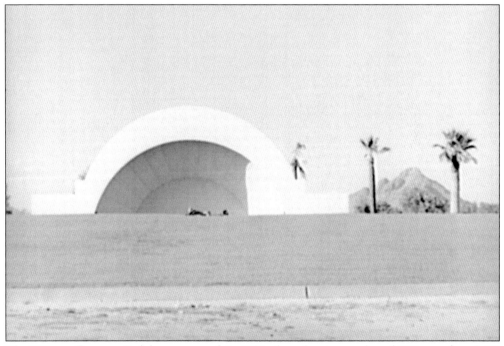

The 222-acre Encanto Park became a park in 1934 when the city purchased 100 acres from J. W. Dorris. The first order of business was to stop livestock from grazing there. Eventually the park included picnic areas, a lagoon, a boathouse, a swimming pool, an amusement park, fishing, and two golf courses (the third oldest golf course in Arizona). Enchanted Island and the Kiddieland Train were popular attractions. Here is a photograph of the Encanto band shell with Piestewa (Squaw) Peak in the background. (Courtesy Heberlee Collection.)

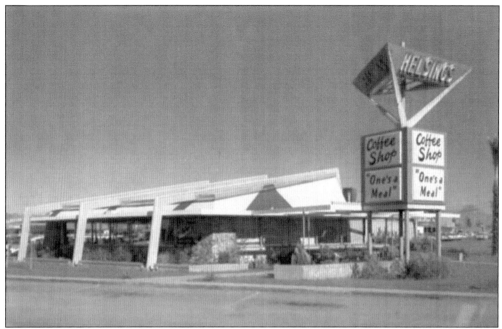

Helsing's Coffee Shop at 2 East Camelback Road was part of Uptown Plaza, the northeast corner of Central Avenue and Camelback Road, in 1955. Uptown Plaza opened in August 1955 and was one of Phoenix's first major shopping centers. (Park Central Mall opened in 1957.) It was built by Del Webb. Helsing's was a popular, reasonably priced family dining restaurant, and Mr. Helsing immediately opened another coffee shop at 245 North Central Avenue. By 1968, Helsing's had four locations: 3402 North Central Avenue, 245 North Central Avenue, Uptown Plaza, and 601 West Van Buren Street. (Courtesy Heberlee Collection.)

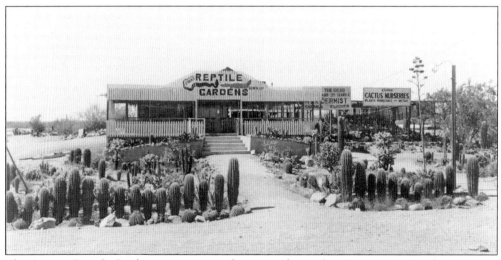

The Arizona Reptile Gardens was way out of town on the road to Tempe in 1930. Chas L. Evans and his wife, Myra, ran the business at 2228 East Van Buren Street. In a related business, Evans was also a taxidermist. The reptiles moved around, apparently, because the Reptile Gardens are listed at 6700 East Van Buren Street in the 1940 city directory and at 5221 East Van Buren in the 1950 directory. (Courtesy Heberlee Collection.)

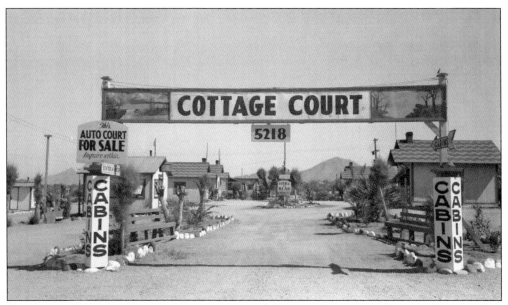

The Cottage Court was typical of the many automobile courts that appeared as travel by automobile became more popular. The Cottage Court was on the Tempe Road, at 5218 East Van Buren Street in this 1940 photograph. In 1950, it was called the Minnesota Cottage Court and was the neighbor of the Evans's Reptile Gardens. Camelback Mountain can be seen in the background. (Courtesy Library of Congress.)

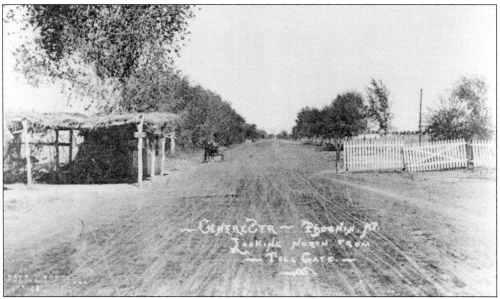

The rest of the images in this chapter give the reader a sense of what Phoenix was like in the past. The Central Avenue Toll Gate was for those who wanted to go north on Central Avenue. The avenue extended northward from the downtown business district to McDowell Road, then continued as a shady, private drive to the Arizona Canal. The drive, developed by Col. J. T. Simms in 1893, was owned by the Central Avenue Driving Association, whose members—the city's elite—and their friends paid a 10¢ toll for the privilege of taking "pleasure spins" in their horse-drawn carriages. (Courtesy McLaughlin Collection, ASU.)

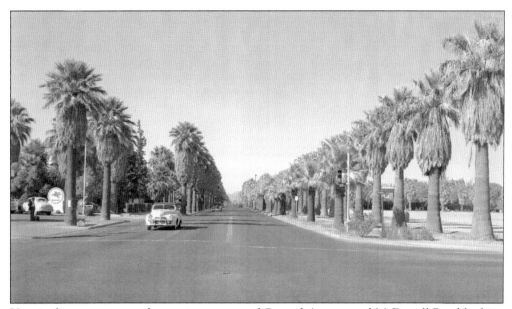

Here is the same view as the previous page—of Central Avenue and McDowell Road looking north on Central Avenue—50 years later in 1948. The 8-acre open lot on the right was land donated to the city by Maie Bartlett Heard in 1940 for the building of a library, art museum, and theater, which was accomplished. The library was opened on March 1, 1953. (Courtesy McLaughlin Collection, ASU.)

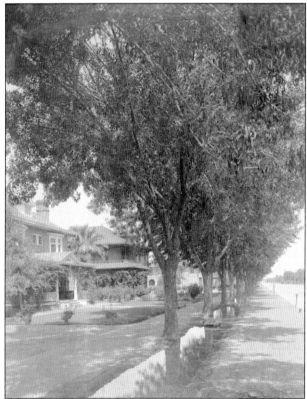

This photograph is Central Avenue, on the west side, with stately manors, large trees, and a small canal passing by in front of the homes. At this time, life was good because Arizona had recently become a state. Soon after, though, the seriousness of World War I set in for community members. The Goldwater House is second from the left at 710 North Central Avenue. (Courtesy McLaughlin Collection, ASU.)

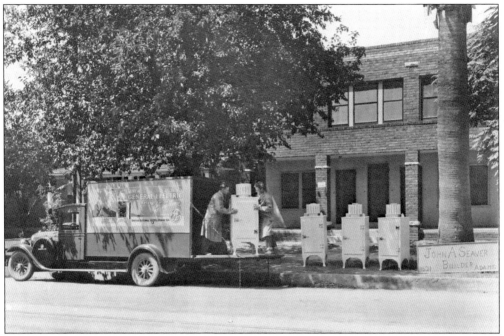

The first refrigerator to see widespread use in the United States was the General Electric Monitor Top refrigerator, introduced in 1927. Pictured here, four refrigerators are being delivered in the early 1930s to a new apartment building at 1621 Adams Street. (Courtesy McLaughlin Collection, ASU.)

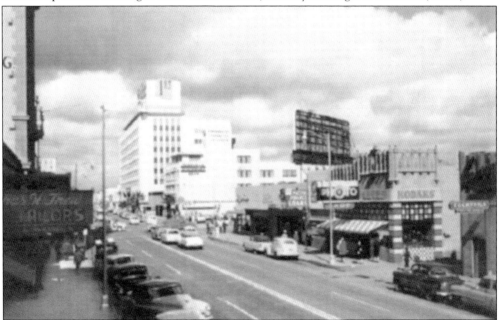

Here is the east side of Central Avenue, north and south of Van Buren Street in the 1950s when it was pedestrian friendly. Retail businesses were located every 10 to 15 feet, inviting people to stroll and see, which is what downtown planners today say is the formula for success. Who wouldn't walk to see the huge camera outside the Kodak color business in that ornate historic building on the right? (Courtesy Heberlee Collection.)

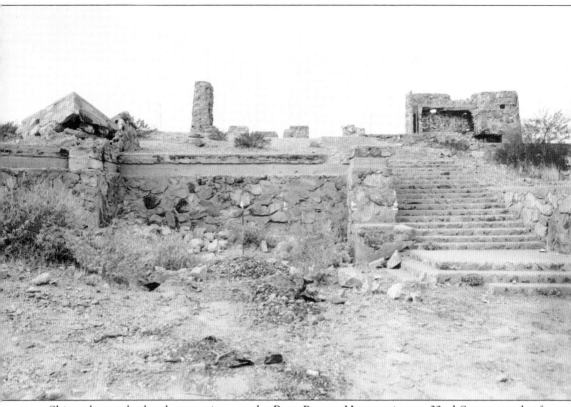

Shiprock was the local name given to the Rose Pauson House ruins on 32nd Street, north of Camelback Road. Thirty-second Street used to go north from Camelback Road, across the canal, and stop at Stanford Drive. The hill at Stanford Drive prevented the street from continuing north. A huge stone house was designed for Rose Pauson on top of the hill by Frank Lloyd Wright in 1939, and the house was built overlooking the city in 1940. (Courtesy Library of Congress.)

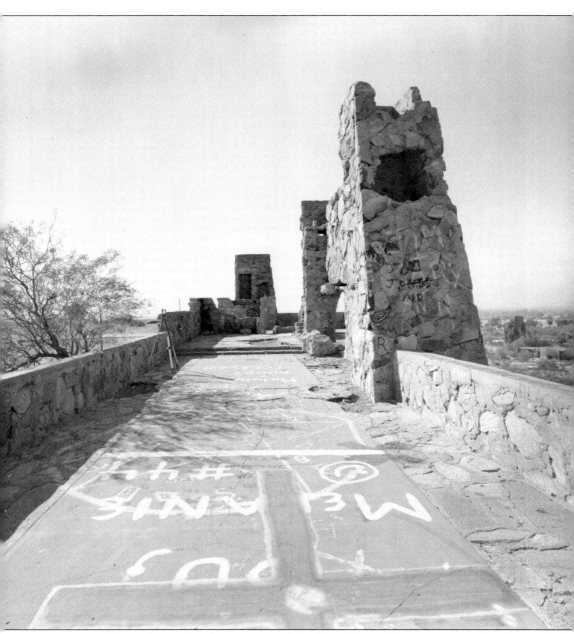

A curtain caught fire from a fireplace ember and the house burned down in 1942. The stone features survived—so the chimney, fireplace, stairway entrance, walkways, and some walls became a mystery place where kids would explore. Thirty-second Street was punched through in the late 1960s. The chimney is still there and can still be seen as the entrance to the neighborhood on the west side of Thirty-second Street. (Courtesy Library of Congress.)

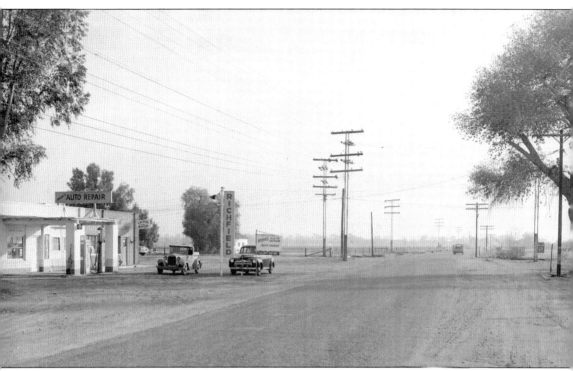

This photograph shows Forty-fourth Street and Thomas Road in 1950. The picture looks north on Forty-fourth Street and the empty field on the left side of the street. The area past the gas station will become Thomas Mall. The mall was Phoenix's second interior mall, and it opened in 1963. It was anchored by Montgomery Ward and Phoenix-based Diamonds. J. G. McCrory 5 and 10 was another popular business in the mall. Businesses shut down in 1987, and the mall was demolished in 1993. (Courtesy McLaughlin Collection, ASU.)

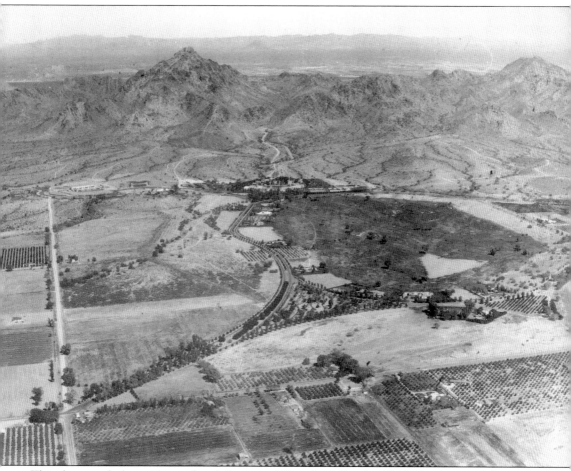

This photograph shows Twenty-fourth Street and Camelback Road in 1946. The Arizona Biltmore Hotel opened in February 1929, and the entrance was originally from the northeast corner of Twenty-fourth Street and Camelback Road. The entrance changed when the Biltmore Fashion Park opened in 1963. The fashion park was the city's original luxury shopping and dining destination. It was anchored by I. Magnin and the Broadway department store when it opened. (Courtesy McLaughlin Collection, ASU.)

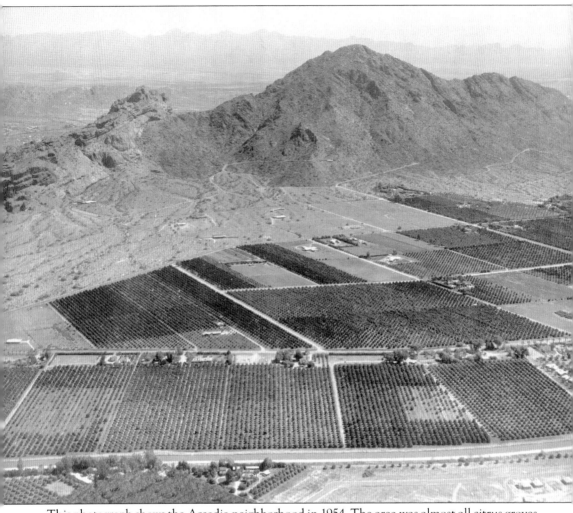

This photograph shows the Arcadia neighborhood in 1954. The area was almost all citrus groves, with about a dozen scattered homes. The Arizona Canal runs along the bottom of this photograph with Lafayette Boulevard above it, followed by Exeter Boulevard, and then Camelback Road. There is almost no development north of Camelback Road. On the bottom right of the photograph, the subdivision of homes foreshadows the future of this neighborhood. (Courtesy McLaughlin Collection, ASU.)

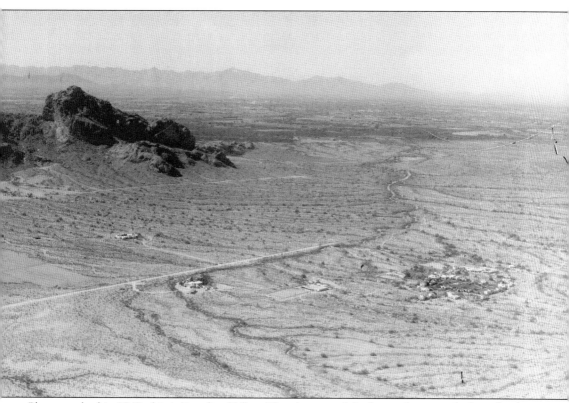

Photographed in 1947, this is Paradise Valley. The photograph looks southwest with Camelback Mountain on the left. John C. Lincoln, the Ohio businessman, acquired unwanted land that real estate taxes were not paid on for around $5 an acre in the early 1930s. Jack Stewart persuaded him to finance a luxury resort in this isolated area. Camelback Inn was the result. The inn opened in 1936, and it was still about the only thing out here when this photograph was taken 10 years later. Lincoln Drive is in the center of the photograph and McDonald Drive is close to Camelback Mountain. (Courtesy McLaughlin Collection, ASU.)

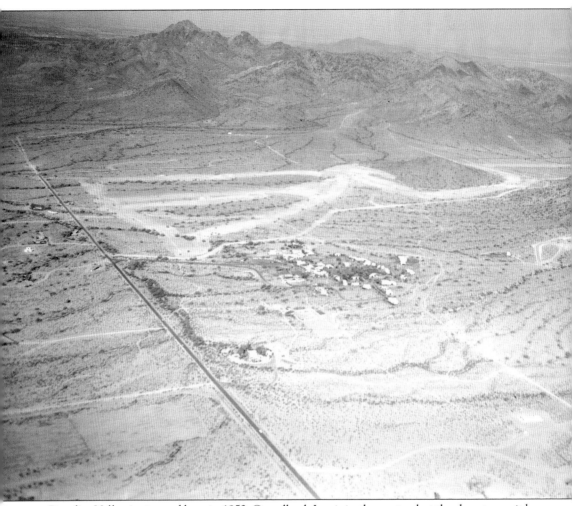

Paradise Valley is pictured here in 1953. Camelback Inn is in the center, but the desert near it has been scraped to make way for a golf course. The photograph faces west with Lincoln Drive at the bottom left. Paradise Valley Country Club and the Clearwater Hills home development began construction soon after the photograph was taken. (Courtesy McLaughlin Collection, ASU.)

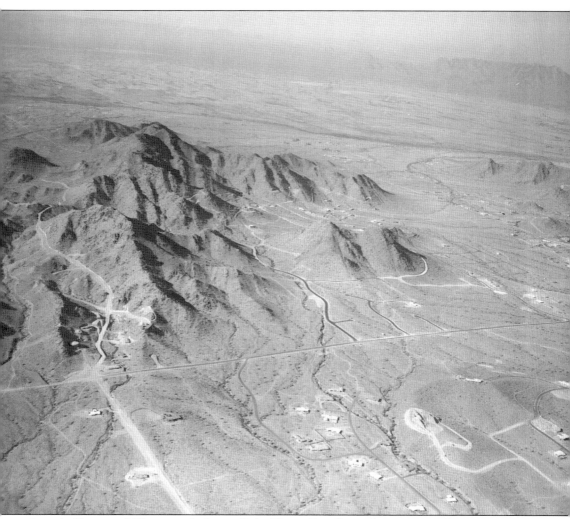

Lincoln Drive and Thirty-sixth Street (Palo Christi Road) are the streets in the intersection at the bottom left in this photograph from 1960. The picture faces northeast, and Thirty-sixth Street goes into the mountains. In the era captured by the photograph, development is slowly beginning to reach this area. Thirty-sixth Street used to be an old wagon or mining road that branched off to a number of mines into the mountains. The road still can be walked today, and it connects to Fortieth Street on the north when it gets close to Shea Boulevard. (Courtesy McLaughlin Collection, ASU.)

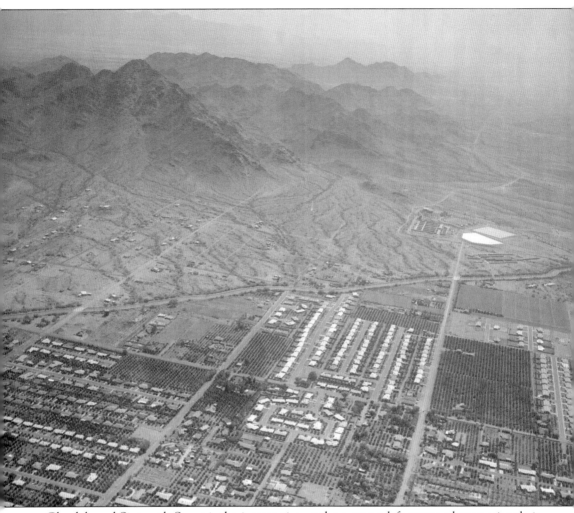

Glendale and Sixteenth Street is the intersection at the extreme left center where a triangle is formed with the Arizona Canal. The photograph looks northeast towards Piestewa Peak in 1959. Lincoln Drive has not yet been punched through to attach to Glendale Avenue at the time. The city's Squaw Peak Water Treatment Plant is the big white area with tanks on the right. Development northeast of the canal will happen in earnest in 1970. (Courtesy McLaughlin Collection, ASU.)

Four

THE FABULOUS FOX WEST COAST THEATRE

I believe that in a great city, or even in a small city or a village, a great theater
is the outward and visible sign of an inward and probable culture.
—Sir Laurence Olivier

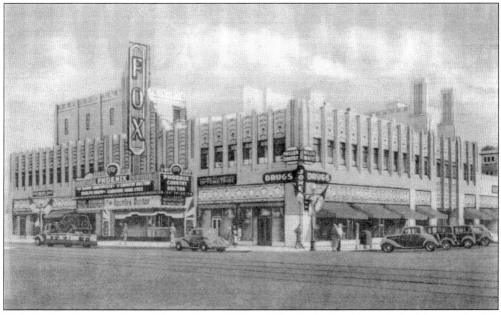

This chapter features the grandeur of one of Phoenix's most beloved historic buildings—the Fox
West Coast Theatre. Not only was it a great building, it produced memories for a few generations
of families in Phoenix who were fortunate to experience the movies and events that took place
there. In this postcard, *The Country Doctor* was released in 1936, and we can see the beauty of S.
Charles Lee's design for the 1800-seat theater. (Courtesy Melikian collection.)

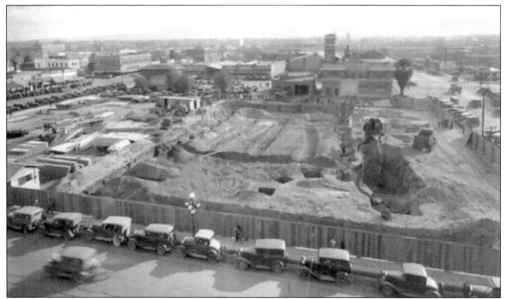

On the ground where the old Phoenix City Hall once stood, in one of the two plazas originally set aside by the founders of Phoenix (in perpetuity) as a place for rest and peaceful contemplation, one of the greatest buildings in the history of Phoenix began to rise in 1929. Here a steam shovel digs out a hole to start the process. You can see Phoenix's first fire station with its tower behind it. (Courtesy Heberlee Collection.)

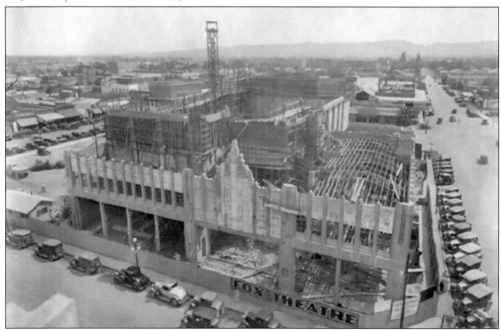

S. Charles Lee was an American architect recognized as one of the most prolific and distinguished motion picture theater designers on the West Coast. He designed one of his largest and most elaborate creations for Phoenix. The result was the magnificent Fox West Coast Theatre at 109 East Washington Street. Here it is during construction in 1930. His Los Angeles Theatre (1931) is regarded as the finest theater building in LA. (Courtesy Heberlee Collection.)

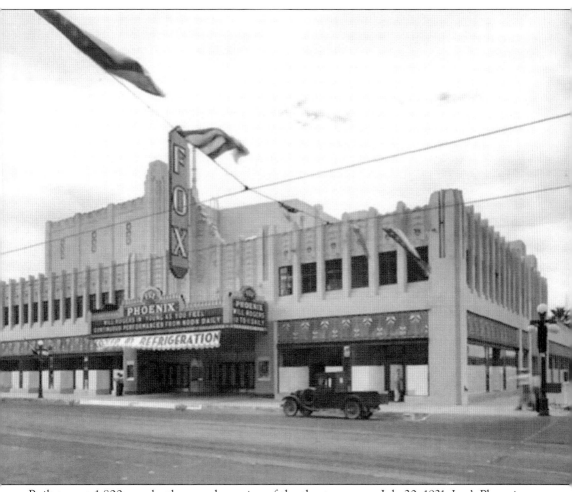

Built to seat 1,800 people, the grand opening of the theater was on July 30, 1931. Lee's Phoenix creation was described to be in the sharp-edged, abstract zigzag art moderne style. In the book *The Show Starts On the Sidewalk Starring S. Charles Lee*, Maggie Valentine describes the sights and sounds of Lee's theaters—huge interiors, crystal chandeliers, art deco motifs, and majestic organ music. (Courtesy Heberlee Collection.)

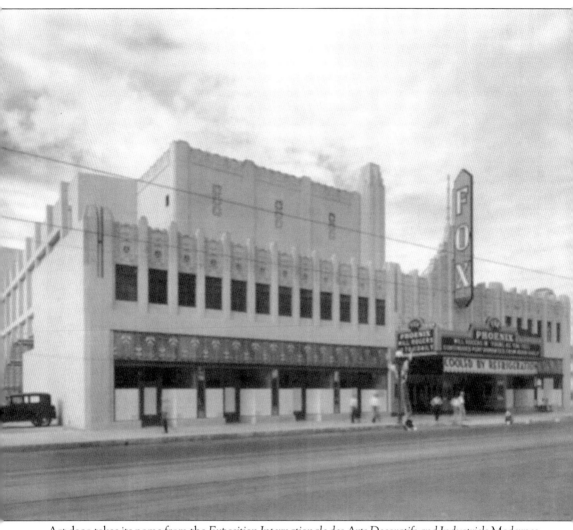

Art deco takes its name from the *Exposition Internationale des Arts Decoratifs and Industriels Modernes,* held in Paris 1925. A showcase for works of "new inspiration and real originality," the style strove for a modern and artistic expression to complement the machine age. An emphasis on the future rather than the past was the style's principal characteristic. Art moderne generally uses horizontal orientation and art deco uses vertical orientation. Here is the completed Fox West Coast Theatre in 1931 showing *Young As You Feel* starring Will Rogers. (Courtesy Heberlee Collection.)

The outside sidewalk had three deco sunburst patterns set into it. The box office looked like a crown and was almost free standing. It stood in front of many mahogany double doors. The outside ceiling was a spectacular blinking sunburst. (Courtesy Heberlee Collection.)

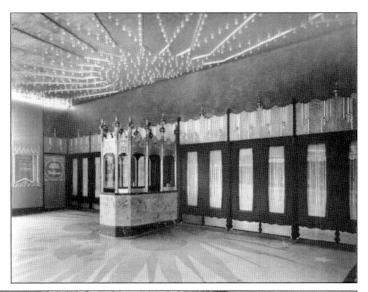

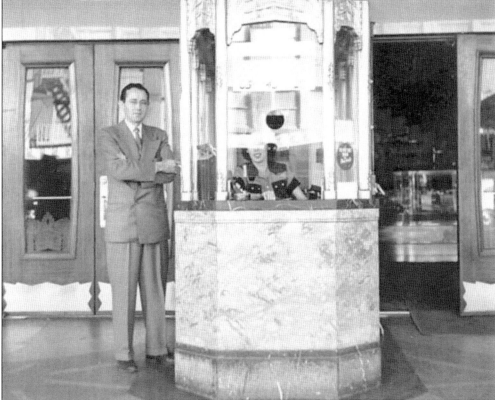

The first theater manager was Albert Stetson. Twenty young girls were selected out of 300 applicants for usherettes. Jo Broddeker, 18 years old, was in charge of all usherettes. Later on in the 1930s, only young male ushers were used because they were regarded as better workers. They wore white coats and ties. In the 1940s, there were male and female ushers. The prices on the box office in this photograph read 65¢, 45¢, and 20¢. Following the same categories as the Lamara Theatre, they are for reserved seating, adults, and children, respectfully. (Courtesy Heberlee Collection.)

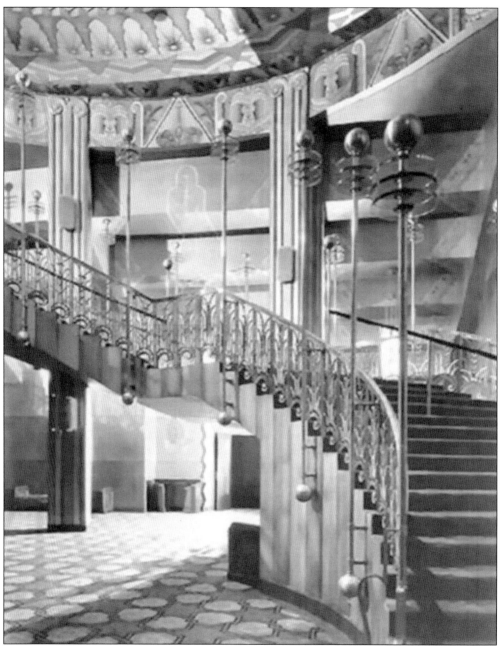

The grand staircase was to the right of the mahogany doors after entering the theater. It had a glistening silver banister curving up to the mezzanine floor. Massive modern pillars supported the staircase and reached the circular ceiling, two stories up. A special feature in the lobby was the row of streetlight-looking metal rods about 15 feet high along the staircase topped by three thick decorative glass disks. At the top and base of each rod was a silver globe about 7 inches in diameter. (Courtesy Heberlee Collection.)

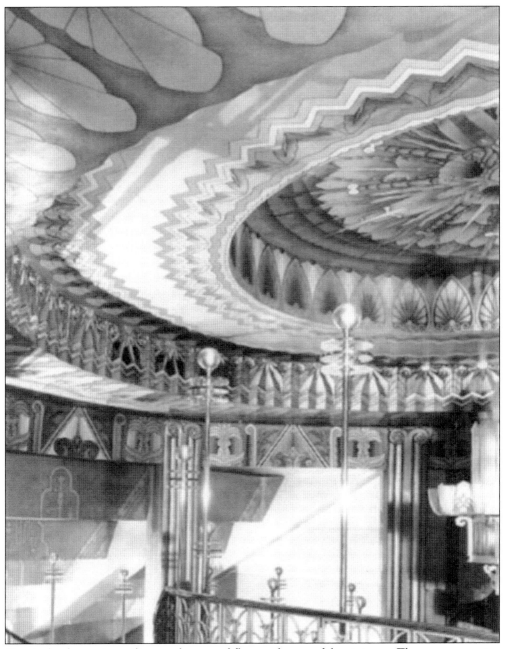

Here is the decorative ceiling on the second floor at the top of the staircase. There was a massive green glass chandelier with 640 bulbs in it. (Courtesy Heberlee Collection.)

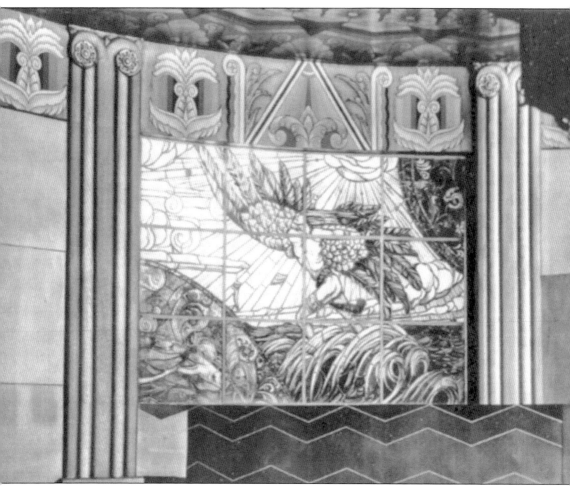

The interior was themed around the archer and the hunt. Here is an example of one of the elaborate figures that were spread throughout the interior—this one is a winged runner from the second floor, possibly a reference to Icarus. (Courtesy Heberlee Collection.)

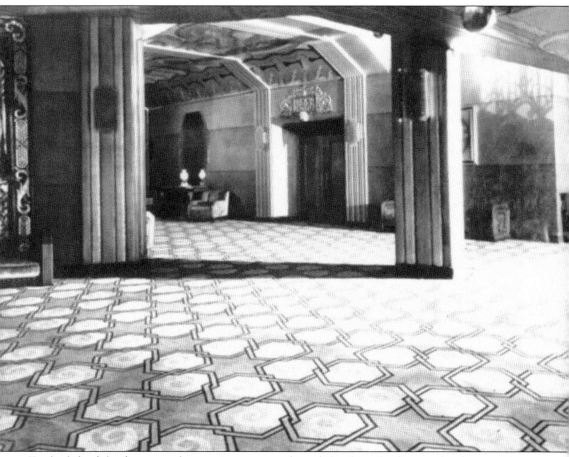

To the left of the foyer was the curving promenade and the doors leading to the theater. The promenade was about 25 feet wide and 100 feet long. At the east end were the offices of the manager. (Courtesy Heberlee Collection.)

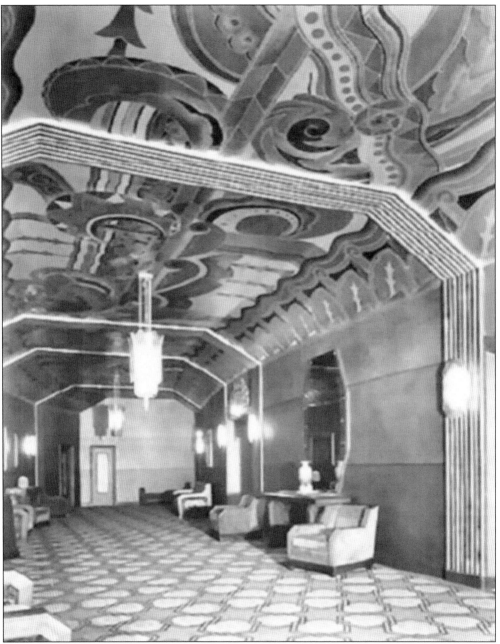

The promenade was a work of art. There were numerous deco paintings of Burmese maidens and deco nudes as well as a massive black marble art deco drinking fountain with a sand blasted design. There were also polished silver balls on each side of the fountain on marble pedestals. (Courtesy Heberlee Collection.)

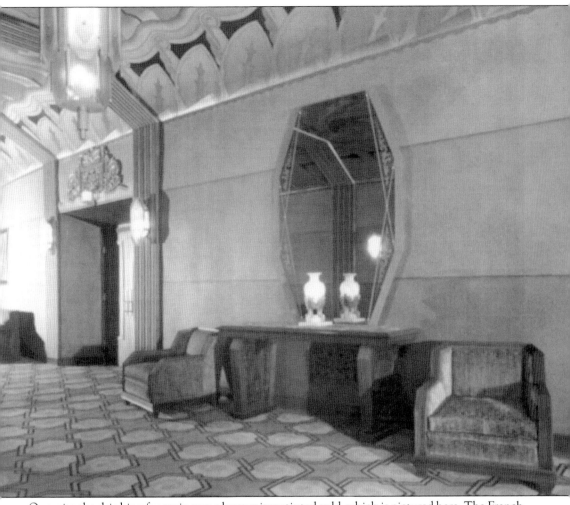

Opposite the drinking fountain was a huge mirror tinted gold, which is pictured here. The French furniture was especially created for the Fox West Coast Theatre and was a mixture of art deco fabrics and dark wood. (Courtesy Heberlee Collection.)

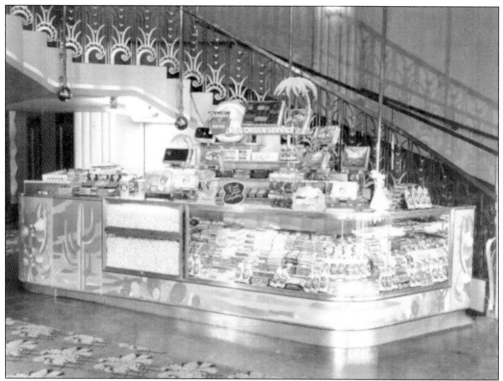

A favorite for the kids was the candy counter, which was installed next to the staircase. The decoration was southwestern instead of art deco. Cacti are depicted on the beautiful chrome and glass structure. In the photograph above, the window-looking display portion is filled with popcorn and the sign reads "Mail Order Service" for its high-class boxes of candy. In the bottom photograph, there are glass bottles of soda in the display case. (Both courtesy Heberlee Collection.)

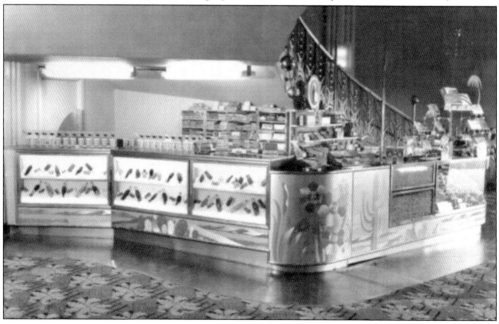

The mezzanine on the second floor had a large lounge with chairs and sofas. There was a railing to one side looking down into the foyer below. A great amount of detail is in the painted wood beams of the ceiling, the horse sculptures, and the art deco tower decoration on the back wall. (Courtesy Heberlee Collection.)

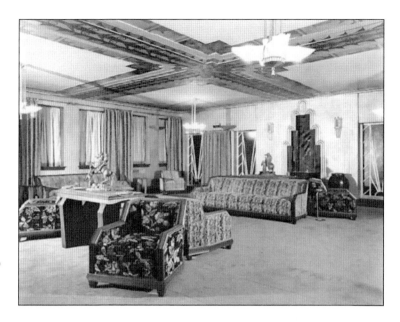

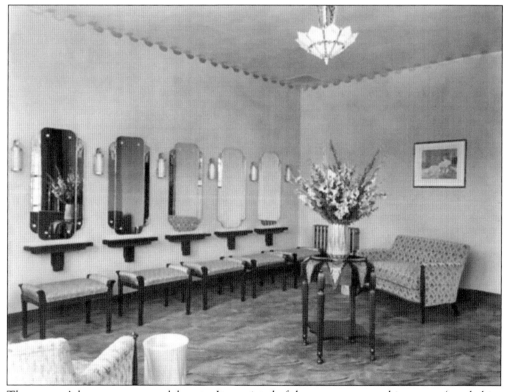

The women's lounge was very elaborate. It consisted of three rooms: a smoking room (two babies were born there); a cosmetic room (above) that had several small mirrors, shelves, and benches, plus one tall mirror that was shaped like a geometric figure eight; and the washroom. The floor was orchid tile. The men's room had a washroom and smoking room. Each bathroom had a pair of large stained glass windows on each side of the door. (Courtesy Heberlee Collection.)

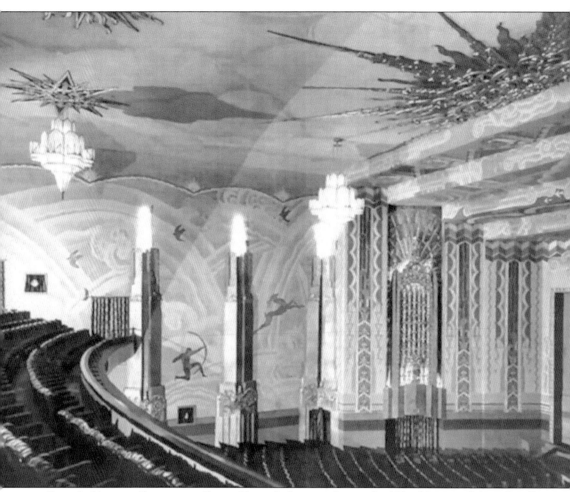

Bas-relief figures of leaping gazelles and hounds done in silver and gold leaf decorated the sidewalls of the auditorium. In this picture, you can see the male archer with his bow and arrow chasing a leaping gazelle while birds fly overhead. This was the east wall of the theater. There was a Wurlitzer thousand-throated organ with massive grilles covered in silver and golf leaf on each sidewall, which can also be seen, and behind that were rhinestone curtains that moved and shimmered when the organ played. The original organist was Walter Danziger. (Courtesy Heberlee Collection.)

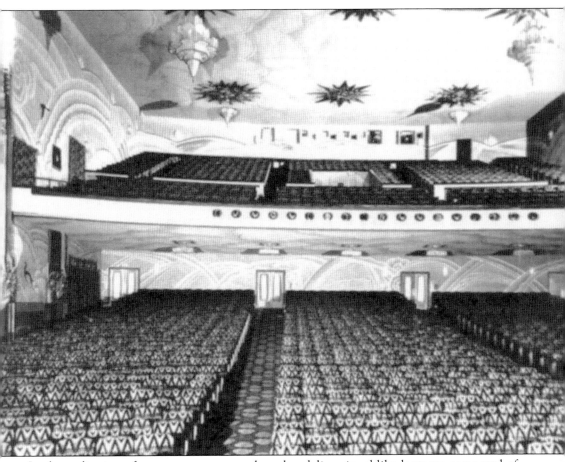

In the auditorium, four enormous green glass chandeliers, jewel-like lanterns composed of geometrically shaped glass panes, hung from the ceiling below decorative stars. The balcony had two smaller ones. The largest of the chandeliers was 14 feet long. There were three lighting effects: blue, green, and amber. (Courtesy Heberlee Collection.)

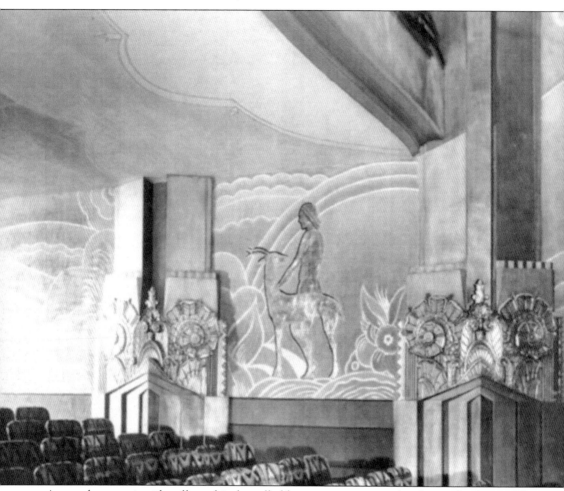

Across the opposite sidewall, mythical gazelle-like creatures romp in the abstract landscape. The walls of the auditorium had stylized skyscrapers like the Empire State Building in heavy silver relief with shafts of blue lights. (Courtesy Heberlee Collection.)

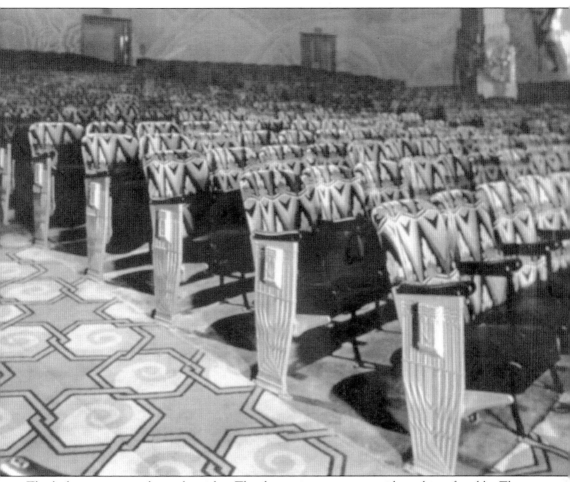

The lush carpet went down the aisles. The decorative seats were wide and comfortable. The theater had 1,000 yards of carpeting. Robert E. Power Studios of Los Angeles was the interior decorator. (Courtesy Heberlee Collection.)

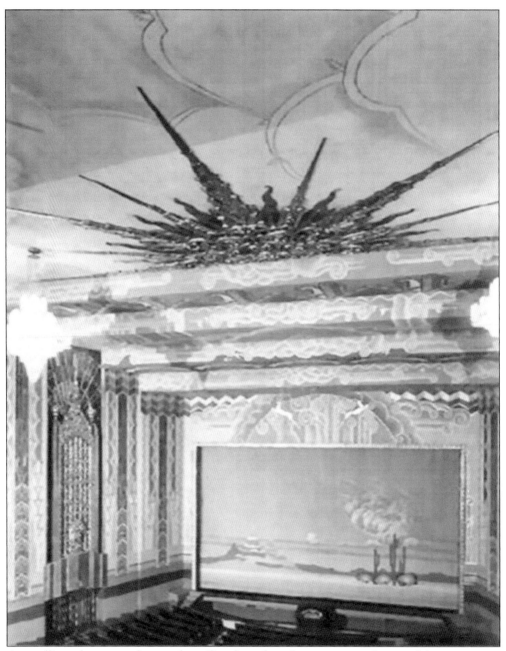

A metallic sunburst spread across the ceiling from the radiating acoustic frames of the proscenium arch in the auditorium. A pair of leading gazelles can be seen above the proscenium. The fire curtain displayed an abstracted version of the Arizona desert landscape. The ceiling was painted with art deco clouds, rainbows, flying geese, and large flowers. The stage was 28 feet deep and 25 feet high. The auditorium was 90 feet wide. In the attic above the auditorium, there was a hand crank to lower the chandeliers to change bulbs. (Courtesy Heberlee Collection.)

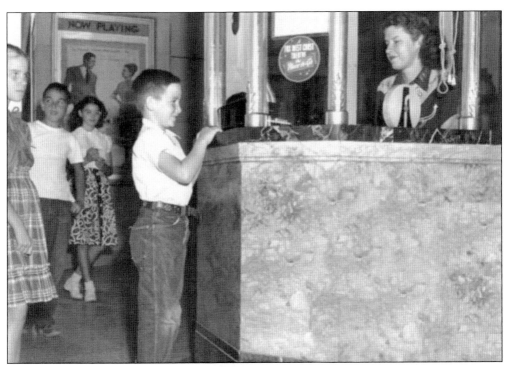

It was a special place for children. When the theater opened in 1931, there was a kids club called the Fox Hunters Club. The club's purpose was to provide children with clean fun and films, as well as talks on how to succeed in life. This was replaced by Lew King's Rangers. A typical Saturday morning started at 9:00 a.m.; the theater would show a cartoon, coming attractions, newsreels, an episode of a serial, and finally the full-length feature. Occasionally children were allowed to see the inner-workings of the theater. (Both courtesy Heberlee Collection.)

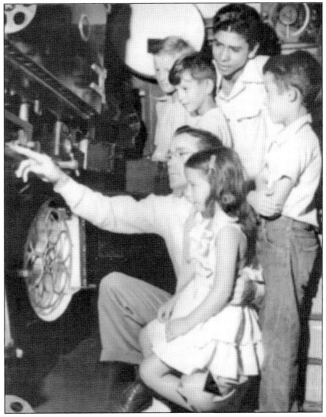

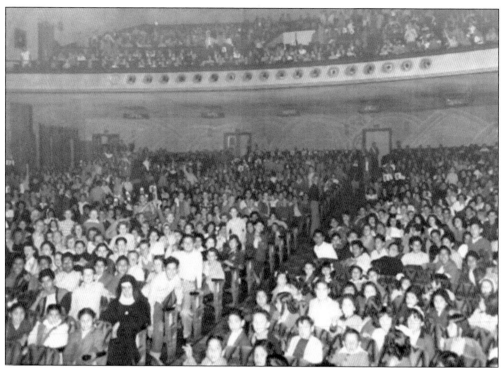

The Fox West Coast Theatre was one of the most important buildings in Phoenix history not only because of its physical beauty, but because it was so much a part of people's lives. Many memories were made in the auditorium. The place was constantly filled with thousands of children and, in this photograph, one nun. (Courtesy Heberlee Collection.)

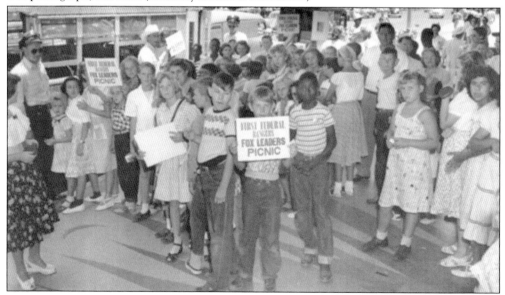

There was even an event called the Fox Leaders Picnic. Buses would take the kids, usually to Encanto Park, for a picnic. Here the children are standing on the deco sunburst pattern in the sidewalk outside the front door, waiting to embark. The sign reads "First Federal Rangers Fox Leaders Picnic." (Courtesy Heberlee Collection.)

Live theater was performed at the Fox. Here it looks like a performance of the *Nutcracker* is going on. The Fox had the first theater air conditioning in Phoenix. Even in the 1940s, people who were not used to the cool air indoors would take sweaters with them to watch a film. (Courtesy Heberlee Collection.)

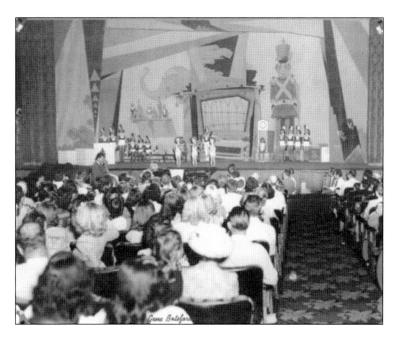

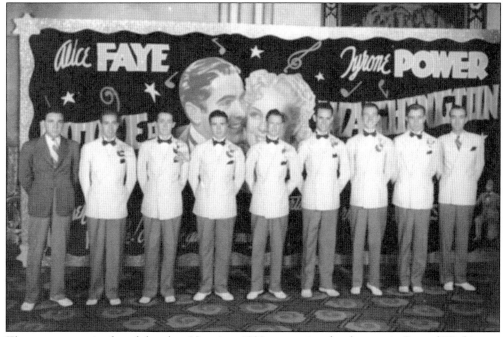

There were movies for adults also. Here is a 1939 promotion for the movie *Rose of Washington Square* starring Alice Faye and Tyrone Power. It was the barely disguised portrait of singer Fanny Brice. Fanny Brice sued 20th Century Fox for $750,000. The studio benefited from the publicity, and this film was its biggest musical hit of 1939. The studio settled out of court with Fanny Brice for an undisclosed amount. (Courtesy Heberlee Collection.)

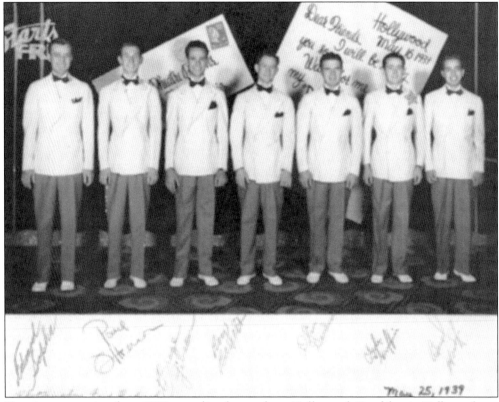

Here is a promotion from 1939 regarding letters from Hollywood. *Breakfast in Hollywood* was broadcast from the Fox West Coast Theatre. *Breakfast in Hollywood* was a popular morning radio show created and hosted by Tom Breneman, who broadcast from 1941 to 1948. By the mid-1940s, Breneman had 10 million listeners. Roderick Smith was the theater's manager in 1940. (Courtesy Heberlee Collection.)

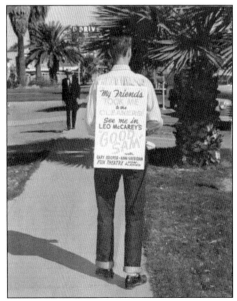

The theater took its advertising into the neighborhoods. Here they are advertising for the movie *Good Sam* starring Gary Cooper in 1948. It was about Sam Clayton, a good-hearted man who likes to help people in need, so much so that he often finds himself broke and unable to help his own family. The Fox catered to families, and it even had an interesting service—if you had groceries, the ushers would put them in cold storage for you. A display case for a movie poster would open up, and behind it was a dumb waiter. They would also use the dumb waiter to take reels of film up to the second floor. (Courtesy Heberlee Collection.)

The Fox Theatre even hosted a national coast-to-coast broadcast. *America's Town Meeting of the Air* was a public affairs discussion broadcast on radio from 1935 to 1956. One of radio's first talk shows, the moderator was George V. Denny Jr., who was the executive director of the organization that produced the show, the League for Political Education. Denny came to Phoenix, and these photographs are from the event in Phoenix on August 28, 1947. The subject was "Can Free Enterprise Here Compete With Socialism Abroad." KPHO and Arizona State College were also involved. The popularity of television led to the broadcast's decline. (Both Courtesy Heberlee Collection.)

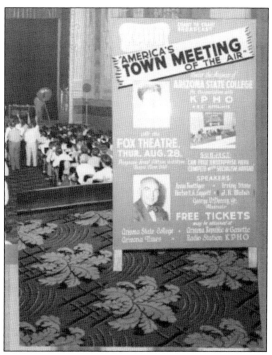

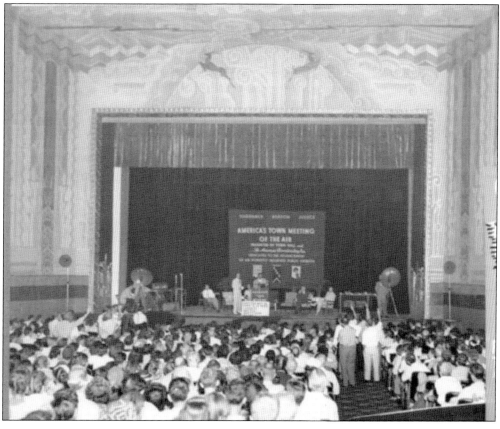

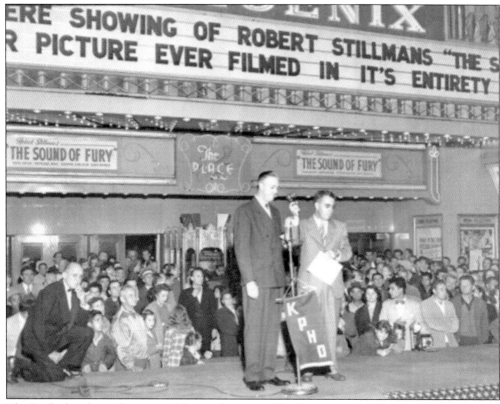

The Fox had its share of premieres. Here is a large crowd for the premiere of *The Sound of Fury* in 1950. It was a black and white film noir starring Frank Lovejoy (center) and Kathleen Ryan. Jack Williams (right) worked at KPHO and was, most likely, interviewing Lovejoy. Williams was a radio announcer who became governor of Arizona from 1966 to 1974. (Courtesy Heberlee Collection.)

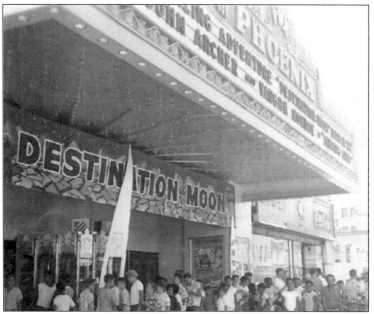

The Fox West Coast Theatre had one of the first science fiction films to attempt a high level of accurate technical details about the first trip to the moon—*Destination Moon*—in 1950. (Courtesy Heberlee Collection.)

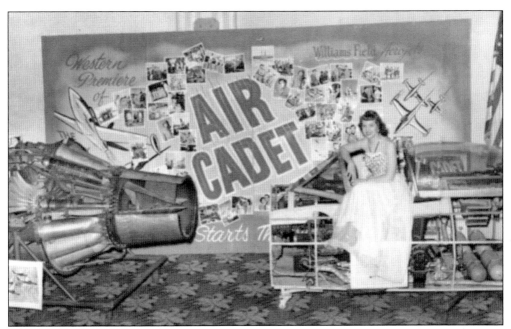

Some films premiered at the theater and came with their own props. The Fox had the western premiere of *Air Cadet* in 1951, which was a movie about a group of cadets and their assorted problems at the U.S. Air Force Pilot Training Academy. On display are a jet engine and a cross section of a plane. The advertisement behind the girl mentions the Williams Field Aerojets. (Courtesy Heberlee Collection.)

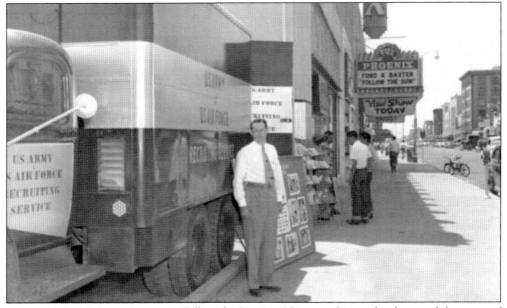

Glenn Ford and Anne Baxter in *Follow the Sun* in 1951 was a biography-drama of the story of golf professional Ben Hogan. The U.S. Army and Air Force Recruiting Service was available on-site to talk to potential recruits. There was a lot of competition in the movie theater business in Phoenix because there were only eight movie theaters in 1940 and the number jumped up to 21 in 1950. (Courtesy Heberlee Collection.)

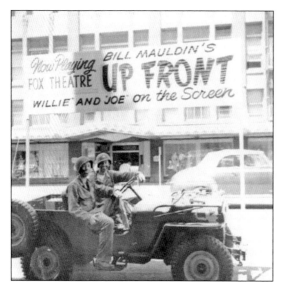

Promotions took many forms, and here are the stars of 1951's *Up Front*. It was based on the World War II cartoons with GIs Willie and Joe on the Italian front. The manager of the theater from 1945 to 1951 was Clyde Griffin. He had started as an usher in 1939 and worked his way up. (Courtesy Heberlee Collection.)

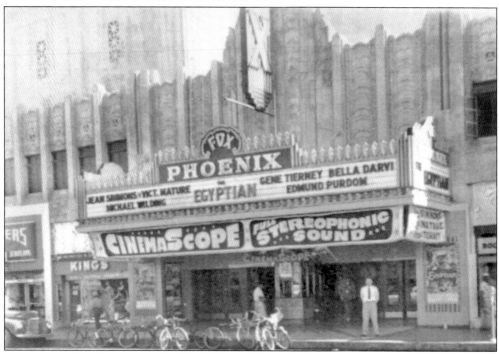

The theater was promoting *The Egyptian* in 1954. It starred Jean Simmons, Victor Mature, and Gene Tierney. Downtown Phoenix peaked around 1957 and the area as well as the theater started their decline as people and businesses moved out to the suburbs. By 1975, the city owned the property and wanted to raze it. There were 18 retail stores in the property, and offices on the second floor were occupied by Dr. Pease, a dentist who had been there for 45 years. The city bought everyone out so they could tear the building down and use the site for the city bus terminal. There was an auction for the contents of the Fox, and the sale brought in only $8,500. A chandelier that cost $8,000 during the Depression brought only $250 in 1975. The magnificent ticket booth went for $280. The author's father purchased metal ceiling panels from the auction and displays them at his business. The theater lives now only in our memories. (Courtesy Heberlee Collection.)

WHY SAVE HISTORIC BUILDINGS?

Preservation helps people, places, our environment, and our economy because old buildings: add to the variety and beauty of our lives, which become more mechanized and stereotyped on a daily basis; are physical links to the past; reflect old values; can be a green alternative to new construction and foster development that is socially, economically, and environmentally sustainable; give many people a feeling of calmness, a sense of security, and a feeling of being linked by sharing similar experiences with their community; foster a sense of unique national and personal identity; have intrinsic value as art; encourage pedestrian activity and face-to-face interaction.It is the blending of the new and the old that makes for a lively, appealing urban environment. Not every old building should be saved, but without historic preservation, Phoenix would become a creeping, spreading mass of architectural mediocrity.

What can be done? The best tool for saving historic buildings is transferable development rights. The city can solve the problem of land scarcity downtown by creating more of it. When a property on valuable land is deemed worthy of historical preservation, the landowner can be granted transferable development rights equal to the potential value of the property on which the historic building sits. Those rights could then be transferred to another parcel of land, even if such a transfer takes the building over the city's height limit. In that case, the historic building is saved, the property owner's rights are not infringed upon, the city gets its additional space and tax revenue, and the overall goal of adding density is met. This process would also allow heights in the city to be increased in a slow and orderly fashion, which is appropriate given growth pressures.

The next step is strengthening the historic preservation ordinance and focusing it on commercial buildings. The city's historic preservation office should have the ability to deny a demolition permit. It should be used carefully, but some buildings are irreplaceable. This is a very important step but a difficult one right now in light of Prop. 207, an unduly restrictive antigovernment law. A property listed on the National Register of Historic Places and the Phoenix Historic Property Register does not stop the property owner from demolishing the historic property—the most that can be done is to halt demolition for 365 days. This must be corrected right away.

Adapt a smart building code, which is happening right now, to make rehabilitation attractive. If an owner wants to keep a historic building standing, he should be given a great deal of leeway. It could be a bad business decision to alter a historic building away from its roots, but that should be up to the sympathetic owner if he feels he needs to do that in order to keep the building economically viable. If an owner wants to raze a historic building, he should be fought tooth and nail, but the best way to save the building is to let the owner turn it into a profit-maker for himself and by himself. This is also the least expensive way for the city.

The city must start early. Once the owner has optimistic plans for huge profits, if demolition occurs, it is much more difficult to convince him, and it becomes politically unpopular. The city tries to do this, but it is hard to know what an owner's plans are. Therefore, historic buildings should be identified and something like a congratulatory letter recorded so everyone has notice of the historic status. Besides transferring development rights and building code help, other ideas include loans, grants, tax credits, tax relief, and finding a tenant for the building.

Perhaps preservation cannot and should not be left entirely to the city. Most of the cities with strong preservation ordinances have them because there is an equally strong nonprofit presence. City staff cannot be advocates; it needs to come from the outside to be most effective. Phoenix should be designed to serve and enrich the people who live there, not to fulfill a market-driven or textbook vision packaged and promoted by real estate interests.

DISCOVER THOUSANDS OF LOCAL HISTORY BOOKS FEATURING MILLIONS OF VINTAGE IMAGES

Arcadia Publishing, the leading local history publisher in the United States, is committed to making history accessible and meaningful through publishing books that celebrate and preserve the heritage of America's people and places.

Find more books like this at
www.arcadiapublishing.com

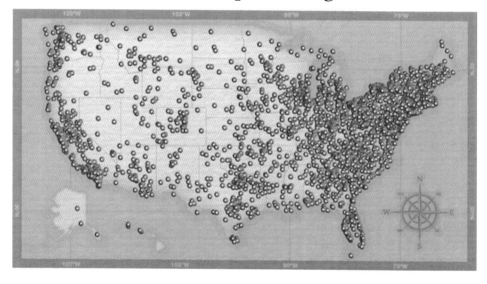

Search for your hometown history, your old stomping grounds, and even your favorite sports team.

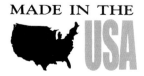